THE REAL
FOOTBALL
FACTORIES

THE REAL
FOOTBALL
FACTORIES

SHOCKING TRUE STORIES FROM THE WORLD'S
HARDEST FOOTBALL HOOLIGANS

DOMINIC UTTON WITH
DANNY DYER

JOHN BLAKE

First published in paperback in 2009
This edition published in 2018

ISBN: 978 1 78606 898 9

British Library Cataloguing-in-Publication Data:

A catalogue record for this book is available from the British Library.

Design by www.envydesign.co.uk

Printed and bound in Great Britain by Clays Ltd, St Ives plc

3 5 7 9 10 8 6 4 2

Papers used by John Blake Publishing are natural, recyclable products made from
wood grown in sustainable forests. The manufacturing processes conform to the
environmental regulations of the country of origin.

Every attempt has been made to contact the relevant copyright-holders,
but some were unobtainable. We would be grateful if the appropriate people
could contact us.

John Blake Publishing is an imprint of Bonnier Publishing
www.bonnierpublishing.com

CONTENTS

FOREWORD

WELCOME TO *The Real Football Factories*. Over the next 250 or so pages you're going to hear about some of the most brutal, most terrifying, most passionate football firms on the planet. You thought we had the hardest, most respected outfits in football? Think again. We went out to meet firms that make our worst look like a bunch of naughty kids: we met their top boys, on their terms, in their manors. And it wasn't always pretty.

We were a small crew – me, a producer, a director and a researcher, out there to film for a TV series you may have seen – but we looked out for each other. There were times we needed to. We were shot at, stoned, chased and tear gassed. We were threatened, challenged, offered out: and we weren't always sure we were going to come back in one piece. We were in Argentina for the last game before the antics of their hooligans forced the authorities to ban away fans from travelling for the rest of the season – and we were in Italy just before the whole league was torn apart and policemen started getting killed. We ran for our lives in Holland and we just escaped a glassing at Galatasaray. We went to see a Serbian firm accused of war crimes and while travelling to a game with a Brazilian firm we came under gunfire from rival fans and had the windows of our bus shot out. In Poland we came close to joining a full-on riot.

We stood on terraces with some of the nastiest firms in the world and we heard about their worst exploits – straight from the boys who carried them out. We got right into their organizations and we talked to their top men.

It was a whirlwind, a proper head-rush. We visited nine countries in 90 days, taking in over a score of firms and experiencing for ourselves some of the most violent football hooliganism on the planet. We had some real laughs – and there were times we nearly shit ourselves too.

This is the true story of what happened – some of it when the cameras were rolling, a lot of it when they weren't. This is the unedited version of events. This is *The Real Football Factories*. We had a blast making it – I hope you do reading it.

Danny Dyer, London 2007

ACKNOWLEDGEMENTS

THANKS MUST GO first and foremost to Danny, without whom, etc. Also all the Zig Zag firm and fixers: Alex Stockley, Ariel Pintor, Ben Barrett, Briony Clark, Bushra Akram, Carl Callam, Dan Riley, Danny Fenton, Denis Karam, Dolores Martinez, Elzbieta Tutajewicz, Fernanda Rizzo, Fernando Cavalcanti, Ivan Katya, Jakub Dospiva, Jonathan Knapp, Katarzyna Porczyk, Kat Wash, Kevin Augello, Kevin Utton, Martin West, Michela Marchant, Mick Kelly, Minna Sedmakov, Miranda Wilson, Nicola Ellis, Oli Parsons, Peter Day, Rana Husnu, Ronaldo Amado, Sarah Pipe, Sophie Ardern, Stephen Koumas, Susie Valerio, Vladimir Novak, Wolfgang Matt. Lastly, Stuart Cooper, Heidi and the one they call The Bean.

This book has been written by journalist Dominic Utton, following extensive interviews with the *Real Football Factories International* crew. Dominic writes for a range of national newspapers and magazines including *The Mirror*, *The Guardian* and *The Express*. For narrative purposes, the character of Stan is an amalgamation of several of the crew who accompanied Danny and Peter around the hooligan world.

CHAPTER ONE

BACK HOME

THEY CALLED IT the English Disease.

In the 1970s and 80s our football terraces were the scourge of the world. Firms from up and down the country, from London to Liverpool, across the Pennines and back again, were feared around the planet.

We brought football to the masses – and then we brought football hooliganism. Crews like the Chelsea Headhunters and Tottenham's Yid Army, the Inter City Firm of West Ham and Millwall's F-Troop, tore up the capital every weekend… and the pattern was repeated across the country, across the divisions. Whether it was the glamour outfits like the Red Army of Manchester United and the Leeds Service Crew, or the smaller, often nastier, firms like Stoke's Naughty 40 or Burnley's Suicide Squad, football support became a serious business. And often a seriously dangerous one, too.

And they weren't doing too bad north of the border either. Ask anyone who's ever run across Hibs/Hearts, or got the wrong side of firms like the Aberdeen Soccer Casuals. Ask anyone who's been to an Old Firm Derby. Such is the passion for kicking off up there, one recent Rangers v Celtic reserves game alone resulted in 184 arrests.

It wasn't just about tear ups on a Saturday afternoon either – it was about fashion, culture, identity. It was a whole lifestyle choice. From the 'casuals' fashion of the terraces – started when Liverpool and Man United fans began fronting up at the weekends in the latest European threads, courtesy of looting sprees on UEFA away days – to ancient notions of pride and identity, for many of the boys being part of the firm defined who they were.

Then again, of course, there were some who were just plain nutters.

It wasn't long before the homegrown hooligans began to look beyond these shores. Europe has always been the prize for our clubs – and so it was for our firms too. Back in the day, English teams dominated European competition – and their supporters were like an invading army, leaving entire city centres devastated in their wake.

Rotterdam, Turin, Dusseldorf, Bilbao and countless others – all of them trashed in the name of football.

Europe reeled; the world looked on in horror; and our firms never had it so good.

Some of the crews became famous, some of the top boys little short of celebrities. West Ham's Inter City Firm even pioneered the calling card, left on those unlucky enough to cross them: 'Congratulations,' it read, 'You have just met the ICF'. In certain households, the likes of Cass Pennant, Trevor Tanner and Jason Marriner became household names; their antics the stuff of legend.

It couldn't last. When boys from Liverpool and Turin

clashed in Belgium's crumbling Heysel stadium one night in May 1985, it didn't end with cuts and bruises. It ended with death: 39 Juventus fans crushed under a collapsing wall as rival fans charged.

UEFA, the British government and the clubs' establishment all declared war on the hooligans. English teams were banned from Europe for five years (with Liverpool serving another year on top of that). There were high profile arrests, undercover surveillance was introduced, all-seater stadiums, CCTV, banning orders...

There were still flashpoints of course. Talk to Trevor Tanner, top boy of Tottenham's Yid Army and he'll happily reminisce about the legendary Ifield Tavern riot of 1991 in which 200 of the Tottenham firm clashed with the same number of Headhunters outside the Stamford Bridge pub. 'The boozer was annihilated,' says Trevor, 'and there was a lot of claret about, know what I mean?'

Throughout the decade, English fans followed the national team across Europe – and left a trail of destruction. Sardinia in 1990, Malmo and Stockholm in 92, Dublin in 95, Marseille in 98, Charleroi in 2000 – all laid waste by the English Disease.

But barring these relatively isolated incidents, it seemed the heyday of football violence was over.

Not quite.

There might not be the action on the terraces of old, but away from the grounds, in the alleyways and parks, on the internet and through underground networks, the firms are regrouping. The market for hooligan books, DVDs, TV shows and even 'audience with' nights with terrace legends has never been bigger. Something's happening out there.

In 2006 we made a TV series, *The Real Football Factories*, in order to take a look at the history of British hooliganism – and also find out how things stand now.

We got Danny Dyer on board to present it – as a passionate West Ham fan and the star of *The Football Factory*, the only hooligan movie to really hit the mark (and, let's be honest, the film from which we lifted the title of our show) he was the obvious choice.

In that series we travelled up and down Britain, from London to Scotland – and we met some real terrace legends from back in the day.

We also met some of the new breed.

We went to an Old Firm Derby and got into the heart of the Celtic terraces – and then skipped across town to talk to a Rangers firm who reckon violence is still very much an ongoing scene up there.

We met young firms in Burnley and Tottenham, boys finding their way around the authorities to kick off in the streets and alleyways around the grounds; and we heard how violence is slowly, steadily, creeping back into football support. Leeds averaged 100 arrests a year between 2000 and 2005 – with 339 banning orders in the same time – and in season 2004/2005 alone, 160 Man United fans were arrested for hooligan offences.

And then we began to hear whispers. If you want to see the real deal now, we were told, you have to look abroad.

Just as we invented the beautiful game and saw the rest of the world take it up and, sometimes, do it better than us; so it seems the same has happened with terrace culture.

Hooliganism has gone global. Firms from Buenos Aries to St Petersburg have taken the English Disease and made it their own. And if some of them are kicking off like it's mid-80s Britain, others have gone way further than we ever did. In Istanbul in 2000, two Leeds fans were stabbed to death before a game against Galatasaray.

We set off to find out just how bad it gets.

In 2007, we started filming for another series of *The Real Football Factories* – but this time we were going international. Danny signed up again, and along with director Peter, producer Stan and a researcher, we set off on the mother of all road trips. Nine countries in three months, around the hooligan world in 90 days.

What we saw out there would make some of our top boys proud. It would make others glad they retired.

It opened our eyes – and over the next 250 or so pages, it will open yours, too.

Welcome to the Real International Football Factories.

CHAPTER TWO

THE BALKANS

The former Yugoslavia has a bloody history – and continues to play host to some of the most feared and fanatical football firms in the world. In Croatia the Torcida of Hajduk Split and The Bad Blue Boys of Dinamo Zagreb regularly have the sort of organized confrontations that old hands in the Headhunters and the ICF could only have dreamed about. Across the border in Serbia, the Belgrade derby will see barneys between rival supporters – the Delije of Red Star and the Gravediggers of Partizan – that make our Rangers/Celtic stand-offs look like teddy bears' picnics.

But there's more. These teams used to be part of one league, these states part of the same country. And when a Serbian side played a Croatian the trouble took on a life of its own, way beyond anything the game has ever known. George Orwell once said football was war minus the shooting… this is a story of football with the shooting. This is the country where the firms stopped messing about and took it to the next level. They took it all the way – all the way

*to war. This is the story of football hooligans who swapped
punches and kicks on the terraces for gunfire on the front
line. And it's the story of how one Delije top boy became a
bona fide warlord.*

This is the story of Croatia and Serbia.

There's a plaque up in Split airport. It proudly declares the
building to have been first opened in 1966. For a crew of
Englishmen arriving with football on their minds it seems
like a good omen. But there are other omens too: look a bit
closer into the history of this place and you'll see that the
airport shut again in 1991. Because of what they call 'the
aggression on Croatia'. By that, they mean the country was
at war.

1991. What was on our minds back then? Gazza, Sonic the
Hedgehog, Mr Blobby. Over here, they were killing each
other – more than 10,000 dead within six months of
hostilities starting. And, according to some historians, it all
began with a football match: Dinamo Zagreb of Croatia
versus Red Star Belgrade of Serbia. The Bad Blue Boys
versus the Delije.

We would be told another story about the beginning of
that war too – of how what was supposed to be a friendly
meeting between the top boys of two rival football firms
went horribly, sickeningly wrong... and how it was the
passions inflamed that day that led to the first shots of the
Balkans conflict.

'We fucked him,' as Johnny, a hooligan with the Gravediggers of Partizan Belgrade was to tell us of that summit.
'You know when you say to someone, we're going to fuck
you? We actually mean it. We. Fucked. Him.'

Battle lines were drawn and football firms from Serbia and Croatia played a major part of that war. Soldiers were recruited straight from the terraces.

We were here to find out just how bad it got. And – let's not pretend – we were also here to find out just how intense things still get. We were a crew of four and it's fair to say that although we knew a little bit about violence, we didn't know too much about politics. But like Danny said: passion is passion, whichever way you look at it. Passion for your team, your colours, your country. The difference lies in just how far you take it. The war officially finished over a decade ago: standing on the terraces of Red Star's Marakana or Zagreb's Maksimir stadiums, it can feel a bit like nobody told the boys on the Saturday afternoon front lines that.

We wanted to meet them. We touched down in the former Yugoslavia on the trail of four of the most notorious firms in world football. We didn't pretend to understand all the causes and effects, the whys and whos and what-ifs of the break up of the former Yugoslavia, or of the war that followed. We hoped we'd learn something of it: but all we could do was go with what we were told. And what we quickly discovered is that the trouble on the terraces, in a strange and powerful way, acts as a kind of mirror for the greater political tensions that tore the two countries apart. For some hooligans there's no difference at all.

The plan was to start in Croatia, then make the drive to Serbia: you have to drive, as planes still won't fly between the countries. We kicked off in Split – home to Hajduk Split, who along with Dinamo Zagreb pretty much dominate Croatian football; it's also home to the Torcida, the oldest organized firm in Europe. Next up would be Zagreb, Croatia's

9

Capital and manor of The Bad Blue Boys of Dinamo Zagreb. It was in their stadium that the first unofficial shots of the Balkans war were fired.

All being well and everyone still in one piece, we were then headed across the border to Belgrade, capital of Serbia and a city shared by rival football teams – and rival mobs. Red Star have the Delije: Partizan are followed by the Grobari, the Gravediggers.

Three cities; four teams; four firms. And a whole lot of trouble for those who go looking for it... or, as our boys on the ground over here had told us time and time again, for those who aren't keeping both eyes wide open. Producer Stan put it most clearly: 'whatever else happened,' he said, 'we didn't want to get fucked.'

The Torcida of Hajduk Split – 'No running, no staying behind'
Situated on a peninsula jutting out over the Adriatic sea, Split is home to around 200,000 Croatians who, as well as happening to have an airport as old as any England trophy, also enjoy life in one of Europe's most beautiful cities. The Roman walls still circle the old town, and in the harbour the yachts of the idle rich moor alongside traditional fishing boats. In the main piazza drop-dead gorgeous women with impossible cheekbones sip Coke through straws and eyeball you over fake Prada sunglasses. They all look like supermodels; the city looks like a holiday brochure.

We should have come here on holiday. We should have come to enjoy the sights, the beautiful women and the beautiful scenery... as it was we were here to meet big ugly geezers with big ugly scars and big ugly tales to tell. We were looking for the oldest organized firm in Europe.

THE REAL FOOTBALL FACTORIES

What were we thinking of?

Still – the mood was upbeat, confidence was high. And no matter what was to come, there was no escaping the fact that the sun was shining and football hooliganism seemed a world away. Danny was confused. 'I feel like Judith Chalmers,' he muttered, strolling through the old town.

Appearances can be deceiving. Sometimes you don't have to scratch too deeply to open a wound. And like your Mum used to say: be careful what you wish for, son, because it might just come true.

Sure enough, the illusion wasn't to last. The prettiness of Split hides a vicious heart: and if you keep your eyes off the girls and the architecture and look around properly, it won't be long before you see what lurks beneath. Barely a couple of streets into the city we started to spot the graffiti. The same word, over and over, like a mantra, or a threat: Torcida. Torcida. Torcida.

And once we knew what we were looking for, it seemed to be everywhere. We followed the trail through town towards the football stadium: the graffiti got bigger, more elaborate. Less like graffiti, in fact, and more like murals, like declarations of territory and belief of the kind you get in parts of Belfast. Whole walls were covered, entire sides of buildings. And along with that one word – Torcida – there were images: most often the red-and-white check of the Croatian flag; and a serious looking bloke with shaggy hair, shades and a football scarf covering his mouth. He looked like a football terrace Che Guevara. One mural declared: 'If I had two lives I'd give them both to you'.

If the painting put us in mind of the Shankill Road, there was one big difference between these and the kind you find in Northern Ireland. This town does not split its allegiances. There are no sides here, no different points of view. It's all Hajduk and it's all Torcida. Peter, our director, pointed at a streetlamp: a closer look showed that even there was the ornate inscription of the city's top firm.

To be fair, Torcida Split are more established and enjoy a greater level of discipline and organization than any hooligan firm in Britain – and in some respects are a slicker operation than many of our official supporters clubs.

We were here to meet their top boys: but with an outfit like the Torcida, you've got to understand their history before you can get into their present.

They were formed in October 1950 before the championship-deciding game between Hajduk and Red Star Belgrade. A hardcore of 113 fans, impressed with what they had seen of the Brazilian supporters at the recent World Cup, had the idea of getting together a similarly passionate group to spur the team on during the big game. They even took their name from those South American fans – it comes from the Brazilian 'to root for' – and the idea was that the fervour, the passion and the volume of the mob inside the stadium would give the players the strength to overcome any opposition. They gathered in the early morning before the game outside the Red Star players' hotel and struck up a huge noise with whistles, sirens, bells and whatever else came to hand… and modern European football support was born.

Torcida Split may be the oldest organized firm in Europe, but these days they don't limit themselves to whistles and bells, a few songs and the odd flare. Torcida Split have a pedigree for violence, too.

The writing was on the wall from day one. On November

THE REAL FOOTBALL FACTORIES

1, 1950, a newspaper article describing the Torcida's noisy wake-up call declared: 'members of this group held... offensive attitudes, which if not stopped would spread hate between the clubs.'

How right they were. And it didn't take them long to flex their muscles. In 1961, barely 10 years after they were formed, they took it to the next level. Following a 1-0 home defeat to Sarajevo, members of Torcida attacked the referee Aleksander Skoric after the game. His crime was to have disallowed a Hajduk goal.

In 1974 they took on the Yugoslav Army. Hundreds of soldiers who had travelled to Split to support Red Star Belgrade were charged by the home firm – and the local boys quickly gained the upper hand over their military opposition. With more and more soldiers going down, it took the presence of a Major – and his gun – to restore order. He did this by evacuating the Army from the stadium altogether.

That victory was to mark a new phase for the Torcida. They were known for their strength on the terraces, their flags, banners, chants and near-continuous songs, the terrifying charges they'd lead against opposition fans... but now they started getting together away from the stadium.

Greater numbers of Torcida were meeting up even when there was no game on. Bars such as Café Dubrovnik became known as Torcida barracks – a bit like certain Chelsea, United, or Rangers pubs on a Saturday lunchtime... only like that seven days a week. Semi-formal meetings were held to make up new songs, new chants, to organize trips for away games, strategies for taking on rival firms, ways to outwit the police. They had to organize away days – because by this time no other fans dared come to Split.

It was also around this time that the graffiti started appearing. The message seemed clear: Split belonged to Torcida, and God help any rival firms who came here thinking any different.

In 1984 Hajduk played Tottenham Hotspur in the semi-final of the UEFA Cup: one of the Torcida slaughtered a rooster in the centre circle in a symbolic gesture of contempt for the London club. UEFA weren't impressed and neither were the Yugoslav authorities. They decided to take action.

The following season a home tie against French club Metz saw the North End – the Torcida equivalent of Man United's Stretford End, or Liverpool's Kop – stormed by riot police. Caught unprepared, the hooligans stood no chance and hundreds were injured or arrested. But far from breaking up the Torcida once and for all, as had been the intention, the ensuing battle with the law strengthened the firm. After that, every fan considered himself part of the outfit. As they now declare on their website – did I mention they were organized? – 'That year in Split a new trend of supporters emerged. Torcida became something very important, even more important than Hajduk. Our graffiti covered the whole city.'

In November 1987 a Cup Winners' Cup second-round match against Marseille sparked another riot: the home fans set off a tear gas canister and in the ensuing panic and stampede for the exits, it's a miracle nobody was killed. Coming relatively soon after the Heysel tragedy in which 39 Juventus fans died when a wall collapsed, the incident received worldwide media coverage. The match was awarded 3-0 to the visitors (Hajduk had been 2-0 up) and Hajduk were banned from European competition for two years.

THE REAL FOOTBALL FACTORIES

In 1990 it was the turn of Partizan Belgrade. With tensions between Croats and Serbs in the former Yugoslavia reaching breaking point, the fixture had been anticipated all season. The streets of Split hummed with the prospect of trouble for hours before the match: and once inside the stadium, the Torcida made it abundantly clear what they thought of their Serbian neighbours. The match was abandoned after first smoke bombs and then fireworks were lobbed at the Belgrade players. Finally, with the North End in a frenzy, the fences were torn down and the fans streamed on to the pitch. Partizan's players ran for their lives; a Yugoslav flag was burned.

A year later those same fans would be fighting again: with guns.

You could say they're a firm with some pedigree then. They're also a firm with the classiest headquarters any of us had ever seen.

The plan had been to meet with some of their boys on our first day in Split: the problem was, we had timed our arrival in the city with the weekend of the biggest match of the season – Hajduk versus Dinamo Zagreb – and it seemed our lads had got a bit ahead of themselves in the run up to the game. Just about the same time we were touching down in the city, they had all gone and got themselves arrested.

We didn't know whether to laugh or, in a funny way, to feel kind of relieved. Like Peter said, it showed them to be the real deal, at any rate.

In the end we hooked up with Jere, a 22-year-old Torcida hooligan, the following morning. We'd spent the evening in the bar sampling the local brew and betting against each others' attempts to hit on the local talent... Jere and his mates had spent the night in the cells. Needless to say, he wasn't in the best of moods.

'They can nick us for almost anything,' he grumbled, when we asked him how it had been. 'And they beat the shit out of you if they catch you too...'

Although he was dressed in pretty standard football lad uniform – the jeans, the white trainers, the zipped up jacket and baseball cap – Jere didn't look like your usual psycho. He didn't smile much (he had just got out of the nick) but he was also a lot more considered in his answers than most hooligans. It felt like he not only cared passionately for his club – but that he had a life outside it. We asked him what he did when he wasn't running with the Torcida: it turns out Jere is studying for an economics degree. He's no mug, then.

The plan had been to stroll through town, taking in some sights, but Jere had a better idea. He wanted to take us to Torcida Headquarters.

This, as it turned out, is not difficult to find. Above a café smack in the centre of town, they even have their name on the door: Torcida, with Coca Cola signs on either side. We filed past old ladies sipping coffee and a man in a suit reading the paper and trooped up the stairs. And if it was slightly surreal seeing the firm's name on the door like they were a legitimate business, inside their HQ was even stranger. It looked like the offices of an advertising agency, or dotcom start-up. Sleek furniture was arranged tastefully around the room, a plasma TV hung on the wall. A helpful Torcida lad with a wide grin cracked open some beers and handed them around. The only clues as to what really went on here – the planning of extreme violence, in the main – was that the curtains were in red-and-blue club colours...

and the walls were covered in glossy pictures of rampaging Hajduk Ultras.

Jere pointed some out. 'This was probably the biggest battle, the worst scenes of violence that I have ever seen in my life,' he said, proudly indicating an image of total chaos – smoke from flares and tear gas partially obscuring a phalanx of hooligans running full throttle for a line of police and waving whatever weapons they could get their hands on, the air full of stones and bottles and smoke. This was the Cup Final riot of 2000: The Bad Blue Boys of Dinamo Zagreb provoked the Torcida by throwing flares across the fences... the Torcida responded in the best way they knew. Thousands tore down the metal fences and pelted the police and the opposition with rocks and bottles. The police responded with tear gas and water cannons. Ono riot and 98 arrests later, the game was abandoned and the stadium closed for four games.

'In 2000, there was a buzz running through the city that something big was going to happen,' continued Jere. 'There was a lot of tension and the police were very aggressive from the start. And just at a sudden moment everything went crazy: the fans started throwing torches and stuff at the police and the police entered our terrace and fighting broke out. Then after the match, fighting continued throughout the city. This took place all round the stadium and in the main street that leads to the city centre. There were policemen charging from small alleys on the side of the street just hitting random people and there was more than 2,000 people fighting the police. It went on for the entire afternoon.' Hundreds of Torcida were hospitalised that day. 'And about 55 injured policemen,' Jere is quick to point out. A year later they would do it all over again.

The Torcida aren't just about kicking off, however. Their role encompasses all dimensions of fanatical support – and if that includes the violent side, it also includes the passionate, but generally peaceful, Ultras, as well as those who aren't specifically looking for trouble at all.

'There aren't classical divisions as you find in Italy where you have people who are just hooligans and people who are Ultras and people who are just supporters,' he explains. 'Here the divisions are a bit blurred so there are people who are only interested in fighting but they will help us with the choreography; and there are people who only do choreography... but they also get involved in fighting.'

Choreography is a kind of super-organized terrace support, involving the synchronised chanting, flag-waving, banner-unfurling and flare-throwing of whole stands at a time. As we would see for ourselves, it's both terrifying and exhilarating to be a part of.

For the moment though, Danny couldn't help posing the obvious question: so when it does kick off, how many of the firm get involved?

Jere looked nonplussed. 'Everyone. There's no running, no staying behind. Split has a reputation – sort of like Cardiff has in the UK or Naples in Italy. It's not the biggest city, but it's very passionate. Everyone sticks out for each other and helps each other and that's what gives us our strength. And everyone gets involved when shit kicks off.'

Given the levels of devotion that the Torcida display towards their club, they naturally expect Hajduk to at least repay them in kind. And if they feel that perhaps the boys on the pitch aren't exactly giving 100 per cent, they have their own methods of motivating the team. When Hajduk were beaten by Irish part-timers Shelbourne in a Champions League Qualifier in August 2004, it was too much for such a proud bunch of fans as the Torcida. That night they broke into the ground and left the starkest of messages: eleven graves, in 4-4-2 formation.

'We put each player's name into the grave, on the pitch,' says Jere. 'I think it sent a couple of shivers down their spines. The players were afraid to walk through the city for a month after that.'

Jere still hadn't smiled, even as he sipped his beer and reminisced about great Torcida victories. This was not only a seriously organized operation: it was a serious operation. The jolly boys' outings and pies-and-beers-and-a-ruck ethos of most British firms couldn't be further removed. We were given scarves and told we were expected to support Hajduk in tomorrow's big match. We didn't dare refuse. As we left, Jere had a final thought for us.

'We're against modern football, you know. Like, creating a festival where people bring their kids and eat burgers. We're against that, the whole spectacle of the Champions League. We just don't want that to happen to our club. We don't want to become a place where away fans can feel like nothing's going to happen to them. Like they can just eat popcorn and wear a Red Star jersey... that's never gonna happen here.'

'Never,' nodded Danny.

'Never,' repeated Jere.

We shut the door behind us, walked back down the stairs, past the old ladies still gossiping and drinking coffees and, blinking, back out into the bright sunlight. Further down the street we could see policemen erecting barriers for the game the next day.

• • •

Jere had told us there wasn't likely to be any serious trouble at the game – the police have learnt through bitter experience that any Hajduk/Dinamo fixture has the potential to get properly nasty if they're not right on top of things – but he also told us to keep our eyes open. Any weak point in the human wall of riot police separating the fans would be punished; any chance for trouble seized. And if there was that chance, he'd be there.

We took a quick circuit of the city the morning of the match. For what seemed like miles around the stadium the roads were lined with columns of riot police, all sticks and shields, black uniforms and helmets. If they gave the impression of herding the fans towards the stadium, they were also formed like a guard of honour and the Torcida treated them as such, taunting as they passed, singing.

For their part, the visiting Bad Blue Boys were keeping their end up: we saw a column of about 2,000 of them filing towards the ground in formation, wedged on all sides by police wary of any last-minute attempts at ambush. We were headed to their place later that day, and duly kept our heads down... the last thing we wanted was to pitch up on their manor and be recognized as sympathetic to their most hated domestic rivals.

As it turned out, the police stood their ground, kept the mobs apart. Trouble was confined to a series of flashpoints around the city centre – a dozen arrests, a handful of hospitalisations, nothing to write home about. The match itself ended two-all – and also contained three penalties, eight bookings and a sending off. By the usual standards of the fixture, a quiet one, then.

We left straight after the game, stuffing our Hajduk

scarves deep into the bottom of our bags. We were headed 200 miles north to Zagreb, chasing The Bad Blue Boys back to their manor.

The Bad Blue Boys of Dinamo Zagreb – The crew who started a war

In Zagreb we were hoping to join the local firm on the terraces for their next home game – a tie against third-placed side Varteks. We were guests of a Bad Blue Boy called Bogdan – who when he wasn't involved in the tastier side of supporting the Croatian capital's team, was one of Dinamo Zagreb's chief choreographers. It was his job to climb a fence and stand with his back to the action, brandishing a megaphone and orchestrating the fans. And as long as the firm decided we were okay, we'd see for ourselves just what that meant.

If Split felt like a Mediterranean holiday resort, Zagreb had more hustle and bustle; it had the cosmopolitan air of a capital city – and, like a capital city, it also held that edge of trouble. If the incredible thing about Split was that somewhere so seemingly chilled could have such an established and violent firm attached to it, we couldn't help feeling that Zagreb wasn't going to hold too much in the way of surprises for us on that score.

We knew about The Bad Blue Boys. They were the crew who started a war.

On May 13, 1990 Dinamo Zagreb played host to Red Star Belgrade. At that time the two teams were still part of the same country, but Croat and Serb nationalistic feeling was growing on both sides: and nowhere more so than among the young men of the terraces. The Delije of Red Star came down in force, marching through the streets around the Maksimir Stadium like an invading army and led by one Zeljko Raznjatovich, a gangster, bank robber and the Delije top man who was known to his followers as Arkan.

The hours before the game saw flashpoints all around the city as The Bad Blue Boys came out to meet the visitors head-on: numerous police charges with batons and tear gas kept the two firms apart. But with each charge it seemed like the home fans came off worse. At that time in Yugoslavia the police were almost exclusively Serb controlled – and for the Croat Bad Blue Boys it began to look like they were being less than impartial in who they dealt a kicking to.

Inside the Maksimir it all blew up. When the Delije started ripping up the plastic seats and lobbing them towards the home spectators on the adjoining terraces, the Dinamo boys went crazy. Hemmed in by riot police, however, they could only watch as the visiting firm tore down the fences and – as the Serb forces simply looked on – laid into the home fans.

It was too much. The whole terrace moved as one against the huge fence penning them into the North stand and as it buckled under their weight, thousands of the Dinamo faithful poured over it and into the police and the rampaging Delije.

What followed was surely the most significant pitch invasion in the history of football violence. For 70 minutes The Bad Blue Boys, the Delije and the police tore into each other on what had stopped being about football rivalry and had become all about Croat versus Serb. Some of the Dinamo players even stayed on the pitch as it all kicked off around them – and when Zagreb's star player Zvonimir Boban spotted a Bad Blue Boy wrestled to the ground and crumpling under the boots of a policeman he launched himself at the officer. The copper went flying, the Dinamo fan rejoined the fight and Boban became a Croat hero.

It was, for many, the beginning of the civil war. As Zagreb daily newspaper *Vecernji List* put it 15 years later: 'The game that was never played will be remembered... as the beginning of the Patriotic War, and almost all contemporaries will declare it the key in understanding the Croatian cause'.

Battle lines were drawn, literally. Following the match, almost all The Bad Blue Boys enlisted in the Croatian army; while over the border in Serbia, Arkan was to make what had been the Delije into the most feared military unit of the civil war. Less than a year later those lads would be fighting in the bloodiest European conflict since the Second World War.

Outside the Maksimir we hooked up with Bogdan: a big guy – six foot four inches big – with heavy features and a crew cut, he looked more than capable of handling himself. But as he showed us what might be the strangest footballing statue in the world, his head remained bowed. It shows a troop of soldiers, guns in hand and Croat flags on the helmets, along with a plaque inscribed with the date of the riot and the words 'For all the Dinamo supporters for whom the war started on May 13, 1990 in the Maksimir Stadium and ended by their giving their lives for their country, Croatia'. Behind them, the relief shows lovingly recreated scenes of the football stadium being torn up as rampaging fans invade the pitch.

'It's for our brave lads who have been killed in the war for our freedom, for the freedom of our country,' explained Bogdan. 'This is everything to us. This is like a church, you know?'

And it is kind of gobsmacking. Think of footballing statues

we pay homage to – Bobby Moore's, Billy Bremner's. They hardly compare: whatever they mean to us, they are, after all, just men who kicked footballs. Nobody asked them to kill anyone. Nobody asked them to die. Even Danny was almost lost for words.

Almost.

'I've seen statues but I've never come across anything like this,' he said. 'You know Bobby Moore is a hero of mine and he died at a young age of cancer and that's a sad, sad story and I'm not undermining that at all but I mean this is something else, this is another level. You know, it goes to, to the extreme. This makes you go like, right, okay, this is serious stuff...

'I've been to Celtic/Rangers. I've heard about Liverpool v Man United and I know all about the West Ham/Millwall rivalries, but that is nothing compared to this. These guys went to war with each other. Not just a tear up in the street for two minutes or ambushing a pub, or injuring a few policemen. They signed up, got given guns and went to the front line. It's like if England went to war with Scotland! I'm trying to get my nut round this one but it's mind blowing...'

All our heads were done in. Here we were, tripping round the world collecting tales of naughtiness and hoping to chat to a few of the more respected firms out there, maybe catch a bit of foreign culture, maybe soak up a bit of atmosphere with some foreign lads... and we were being asked to consider the fact that such was the passion these lads had they were prepared to fight and to die for the cause. It was humbling.

Stan said that The Bad Blue Boys must be like the Chelsea Pensioners – and we laughed, but then we thought: if the

Chelsea Pensioners had started their military careers running with the Headhunters then perhaps, yes, the analogy isn't so flippant after all.

Bogdan wasn't laughing. He eyed us carefully; he wanted to know what a Chelsea Pensioner was. When Peter explained that they were honoured soldiers (and not ageing fans) he nodded. 'It's very emotional,' he said, slowly. And it seems like right there we passed some kind of test because he told us to meet him again before that night's Varteks match. He'd get us in.

Before then, however, Bogdan wanted to bring us up to date with the current form of his crew. Sure, The Bad Blue Boys had an awe-inspiring history, but Bogdan wanted to show us that there was more to them than statues. They had another side. The present activities of the Zagreb firm might not be so highly honoured... but they can certainly compare for straight-up violence.

Formed in 1986, they took their name from the Sean Penn film *Bad Boys* – but it's best not to laugh when you're told this, because, as well as kick-starting a whole civil war back in the day, their recent history has shown them to be as vicious as any firm in Europe.

In 1994 they earned their team a year's ban from all European competitions after a Cup Winners' Cup game in Auxerre descended into a riot in which several policemen were seriously injured. Three years later they repeated the trick in Zurich, when they took over most of the downtown area after a UEFA Cup match, smashing dozens of vehicles and looting scores of shops. The following year an Ajax fan was stabbed during running street violence before a Champions League game.

In 2000 The Bad Blue Boys took Milan: fighting on the terraces spilled over into the town, resulting in a hardcore of 200 of the Dinamo firm storming the city centre and holding the Italian police at bay for hours. One quarter of that mob were arrested, the same number injured on both sides.

And then of course there's the local trouble, the enormous dust-ups with their Torcida rivals: but that happens so often it barely makes the papers any more.

The passion isn't limited to what's happening off the pitch either. Bogdan explained that although their philosophy is to support the team for the full 90 minutes 'no matter if they are losing 5-0 or if they're winning', after the game The Bad Blue Boys are more than capable of a bit of player motivation themselves.

Around the time of the Cup Final riots against the firm from Hajduk Split, some of the senior Bad Blue Boys felt the team weren't showing the required level of commitment to the cause. Some of the players' cars got trashed, some punches were thrown. 'It was like a yellow card to make them think about where they play,' said Bogdan. 'They are playing for the best Croatian club and the pride of the whole nation, it's unacceptable for them to play like they are at some village club.'

On another occasion it was felt the players didn't have the 'heart and motivation' to be playing for Dinamo. Fifty of The Bad Blue Boys paid the team a visit.

'We decided to go to the training,' explained Bogdan, 'we put them in a line and we took off their shirts, their pants, everything.' After they had stripped the players naked and lined them up, they told them their clothes would be returned when it was felt they deserved to wear the colours of Dinamo Zagreb again. 'We told them, when you start to prove that you are a player for our club we will return your shirts. You don't need to be champions but just show your hearts. Play like men and you'll have no problems with us.' He grinned. 'They played better after that.'

So powerful are The Bad Blue Boys, in fact, that in 1993 when club president Franjo Tujdman – who also happened to be president of Croatia – changed the name from Dinamo to Croatia Zagreb, they set fire to his director's box. 'It was a disaster that year,' says Bogdan, 'we had 1,200 people arrested'. Needless to say, the name was changed back.

We looked at each other. 'Glazer,' Stan said. 'Abramovich. Magnusson.' Somehow, and no matter how good an idea it might seem, we couldn't see disgruntled United, Chelsea or West Ham fans burning down their directors' boxes. Come to that, we couldn't exactly imagine taking 50 tooled up lads into training and teaching our players a little about heart and motivation – although Peter offered to give Bogdan a long list of those needing it should he ever get the chance. Bogdan shrugged, 'sure,' he said, 'maybe your national side could use it, eh?'

We laughed but Bogdan didn't crack a smile. 'Fuck me,' said Danny, 'he's only serious!'

'Well why not?' said Stan. 'Hold up and I'll get a pen…'

•   •   •

We left Bogdan at the stadium with the promise we'd be back in club colours for the night's game. 'You looking forward to this?' asked Stan. 'Ninety minutes on the terraces in the heart of The Bad Blue Boys?'

Danny grinned. Dead fucking right we were! We were itching to get a taste of the kind of passion English football seemed to forget years ago.

Inside the Maksimir that night the din was incredible. The smoke from countless flares hung like a heavy curtain over the stands and stung the eyes, the riot police lining the running track below us subject to a constant stream of missiles. The volume was a steady roar – every chant, every song, every arms-above-the-head handclap perfectly synchronised and choreographed by the boys with the megaphones.

Chants would be started and Bogdan and the other ringleaders, balanced precariously halfway up the fences with their backs to the pitch, would scour the singing crowd, eyes scanning every face, searching for anyone not displaying enough passion. You wouldn't want to be caught like that... and God help you if you're caught yawning, checking your watch, or tucking into a prawn sandwich.

Packed into the terrace we were part of the mob and there was nothing we could do except join in. Not that we would want to do anything else: there was no room here for cautious support or half-hearted belief. This was full-on passion, all or nothing. 'It's sing your heart out or fuck off and never come back,' as Peter put it. 'And watch yourself on the way out, too.' Standing there, carried forwards and then back by the swell of the crowd, lost in the mob and just having to roll with it, was both terrifying and exhilarating. It was weird – like the terraces used to be before the days of all-seating, when dangerous numbers would be crammed in together... but with an edge of delirious continental lunacy that the choreography gave.

The flares were constant: always blue, always lit – Bogdan

28

reckoned they could get through hundreds in a game – and often thrown towards the pitch or the police. They would have been lobbed towards the Vartek fans... except there didn't seem to be any. And that was the weirdest thing of all. The Bad Blue Boys were in full voice, going full tilt – and there was no one to sing back at them.

In fact, aside from the Dinamo faithful, the stadium was all but empty. There we all were, hemmed in at one end, giving it like we were in the Cup Final to end all Cup Finals – and the rest of the ground looked like a pre-season reserves game.

And that's when it hit us: all that passion, the flares and banners and songs... it wasn't to front up to opposing fans, like British firms do. Aside from the Torcida, the occasional foreign firm on a UEFA jolly or the odd lunatic upstart crew, there was no one to front up to. No one comes to Zagreb, no one dares take them on anymore. And now all that passion, all that intimidation... it's to make a point to the players, to the club itself.

Bogdan's choreography, the incredible show of support for a game nobody else bothered turning up for, the threats to the players, the torching of the director's box... to our eyes at least it all added up to one thing. Dinamo Zagreb is a club that the firm went to war for – and now it's a club the firm feel they own.

● ● ●

We left Croatia on the road they used to call the road of Brotherhood and Unity, headed across the border to Serbia and its capital Belgrade. We were only halfway through our Balkans trip and we were knackered. If the sheer levels of tradition and organization that the hooligans of Hajduk Split displayed wasn't enough of an eye-opener, the passion of The Bad Blue Boys – the firm that feels more powerful than its own football club – left us exhausted. Just handling the Varteks game, keeping up with the singing, avoiding the searching eyes of the choreographers, was hard enough. Factor in the whole emotional impact of the Dinamo v Red Star riot that sparked a civil war and we'd been left in bits.

And now we were headed to hear the rest of the tale, to see the Serbian side of things. And, although we wouldn't manage to do everything we originally hoped for in Belgrade, we would end up hearing the most hardcore story of one-on-one football violence any of us had ever come across.

It's less than 10 years since Belgrade was bombed by NATO forces in an attempt to topple president Slobodan Milosevic – and only seven years after nearly a million of them took to the streets to finish the job properly. The scars are everywhere; we'd turn a corner and come across a monument to 15 workers blown up when the TV station was hit; a stroll through a park would end at another memorial – this time to children who were killed when a stray bomb caught them playing. For three months in 1999 NATO battered the city. It all happened so recently: some of those kids wouldn't even be 18 years old yet.

The city also feels a lot more like Eastern Europe than anything in Croatia: Serbia uses the Cyrillic alphabet and many of the buildings have got that blank, imposing Communist feel to them. And historically at least, the same could be said of Belgrade's two football teams.

Both were formed immediately after the war in 1945 by the ruling Communist government – and both created out of an intense and vicious rivalry. Partizan Belgrade were controlled by the Army; Red Star Belgrade by the Secret Police.

These days it's all about the rival firms – and they're every bit as ruthless as anything in the clubs' histories. The two grounds are literally around the corner from one another – and that means that on derby days the whole city can once again become a war zone – with attendant loss of life.

There is no love lost between the Delije (which roughly translates as 'heroes') of Red Star and the Grobari, or Gravediggers, of Partizan. Theirs is a rivalry every bit as vicious as we'd seen in Croatia – only amplified by the fact that they share the same city. And clashes between them have become legendary.

The Delije of Red Star Belgrade – From terraces to Tigers
The game on 14 October 2000 in Red Star's Marakana stadium was typical: the visiting Grobari kicked things off by ripping up the seats and tossing them over the fences at the pitch – as well as firing an improvised artillery barrage of fireworks over to the Delije terraces. Of course, the home firm weren't going to just stand and take that, and hundreds broke through the fencing and raced right across the pitch to where the rival hooligans, who had likewise torn down their fencing, were waiting. Riot police steamed in, players scattered – with several Partizan players sustaining injuries – and the ensuing three-way battle continued in and around the stadium for the rest of the afternoon. Afterwards the Partizan management declared: 'there have always been minor and larger incidents in the last 50 years of play between Partizan and Red Star but what is new is that the fans this time attacked the players and the management

rather than fans from the rival group. Our players and coach were beaten up while entering the tunnel by fans.'

Which sounds a bit like they're saying it's okay when the hooligans kick the shit out of each other... so long as 'players and management' don't get caught in the crossfire.

More recently, a teenage Partizan fan was stabbed just a few months before our visit. Knowing that the Belgrade riot police were going to be all over the area around the stadium before the match, the two firms had organized a get-together on the outskirts of the city. Dozens turned up on both sides, wielding knives, baseball bats, stones, or just relying on their fists. In the ensuing mayhem 12 people were arrested... but not before 17-year-old Aleksander Panic was killed. Some thought it payback for an incident in a previous derby where a 17-year-old Red Star supporter was struck in the chest by a firework fired from the Grobari terraces. He too died.

In the 60-odd years since the army and the secret police formed rival sides in Belgrade, there has only been one significant event that has seen the city's two firms put aside their differences: and it happened on 22 March 1992 at the Marakana. Yugoslavia had disintegrated; Serbia and Croatia were at war, but despite the obvious hatred between clubs of the two countries, older rivalries still prevailed. The Belgrade derby still saw Delije and Grobari hooligans clashing on the streets outside the stadium – and in the cauldron of the Red Star ground, the terraces buckled and swayed as the two mobs let fly at each other, first with taunts, and then with whatever else came to hand.

And then... there was quiet. Everyone stopped – the crowd, the hooligans, even the players – as a squad of Serbian soldiers dressed in the full uniform of the notorious

Tigers paramilitary group ascended the North Stand. One by one and in eerie silence they held up road signs of Croat towns that had fallen to the Serb army. The last one read: Welcome to Vukovar.

Vukovar was a town on the border that had been under siege for nearly three months, in the process suffering the worst devastation of any European city since the Second World War. More than 2,000 Croat men were killed defending it; and when they finally broke through the defences, it's alleged the invading Tigers stormed the hospital, rounded up the wounded and summarily massacred them too.

As the crowd digested the significance of these signs, a lone figure all in black emerged from high in the Delije stand: Zeljko Raznjatovich, also known as Arkan, commander in chief of the Tigers, director of the Red Stars Supporters Association, hooligan and warlord. The crowd – Delije and Grobari alike – erupted. The game was forgotten: the event had become a rally, a call to arms, an expression of nationalism, pride and hatred. The moment is still celebrated as the greatest display of hooligan power in the country's history.

And, if you're of a mind to celebrate such things, Arkan is almost certainly the most notorious leader in the history of any firm anywhere in the world.

Arkan began his career as a teenage bag-snatcher on the streets of Belgrade in the 1960s, but soon upgraded to bank robbery – racking up convictions in Belgium, Holland and Germany and arrest warrants in Sweden and Italy. After he escaped from jail – twice – in first Belgium then Holland, there were whispers that perhaps he had powerful links to shadier elements in the Yugoslav government.

He returned to Serbia in the 80s, opening a patisserie as a

front for numerous illegal businesses, and built an enormous marble house for himself – directly opposite the Red Star stadium. As the political situation in Yugoslavia disintegrated, he took charge of the Red Star official supporters club and quickly rose to be top man in the Delije, harnessing their passion and hatred, moulding it into something he could use, creating an army of hooligans. He later said: 'We trained fans without weapons. I insisted on discipline from the very beginning. You know our fans – they're noisy, they like to drink, to joke about. I stopped that in one go. I made them cut their hair, shave regularly, not drink. And so it began.'

On 11 October 1990, just five months after the defining Delije trip to Dinamo Zagreb, Arkan rechristened his Delije the Serb Volunteer Guard – a paramilitary group also known as the Tigers. Arkan had taught them to put aside their differences with the Partizan rivals and direct all their hatred against what he called the enemies of Serbia.

For five years the Tigers were the most feared militia of the Balkans war. At their peak they were 10,000 strong – and as well as carrying out the massacre at Vukovar, they were accused of some of the most brutal ethnic cleansing of the conflict. Arkan was vilified in the western press as a madman, a monster. To the Delije, however, he was a hero: one of them, a hooligan who had gone all the way.

After the war, in June 1996, Arkan took over the second division team Obilic – and transformed them into one of Serbia's top sides. They were promoted in his first season in charge and the following year took the League Championship after losing just one game all season. Rumours abounded, however, that it was less to do with the quality of their football, and more down to the fact that every game would see thousands of former Tigers and Delije line the terraces, sometimes aiming guns at the opposition players. On one occasion Arkan is said to have paid a visit to the away dressing room at half-time. The opposing centre forward was told he would be shot in the knee if he ever scored against Obilic again.

UEFA duly banned the club from European competition.

Arkan's ambition extended further than Obilic, however. The boy who made the Delije the only firm ever to be indicted for war crimes had his eye on the bigger prize. He wanted Red Star for himself; and he knew that controlling that club would make him among the most legitimately powerful football businessmen in Europe. The club desperately held off his advances and president Slobodan Milosevic was once asked why he didn't do something about Arkan. 'I'm afraid of him,' came the simple reply.

Someone else did do something. In January 2000 Arkan was shot 38 times as he sipped coffee in the lobby of Belgrade's Intercontinental Hotel. At his funeral thousands of former Delije dressed in full Tigers uniform turned out. In the rest of the world he was condemned as a war criminal.

Naturally, we wanted to meet the Delije. Still among the most frightening outfits you never want to see lined up on a terrace opposite you, their history under Arkan is beyond our comprehension. They were a firm who not only became an army, but mobilised into one of the most terrifying paramilitary units Europe has ever known.

There was only one problem. The Delije didn't want to meet us. It can be tricky being a journalist sometimes – sure, the job opens up doors occasionally, it gets you into some places you shouldn't be, puts you behind some barriers and locked doors and police cordons... but it also carries a stigma. The fact is: some people just hate journalists.

We had a local crew trying for six weeks before our arrival to get us an introduction to the firm. The firm had a meeting; they got back to our fixers. We were told: no chance. The Delije had talked to British journalists before – and they were sick of being cast as war criminals. They didn't trust us.

What did we think? To be honest, we thought this a bit arrogant of them. After all, everyone else had talked to us. What made them special? Yeah, we wanted to talk about Arkan, of course we did. How could we meet the Delije and not talk about Arkan? But we weren't in Serbia to judge anyone: all we could do was report what we were told, say things as we saw them. And without the cooperation of the firm, we'd be left with the official, non-Delije sanctioned, version of events. Like Peter said: 'if they're unhappy with what we might say about them, they should come out and tell us what we should be saying instead. Why should they be different to everyone else?'

We asked local reporters if we could try to convince the firm to meet us ourselves. We were told: don't be so fucking stupid. Belgrade is different. If the Delije say they don't want to meet you, if the Delije say they don't trust you, then you do the smart thing and walk away.

We walked away.

We walked across town, into the inviting arms of the Grobari, the Gravediggers. The boys from Red Star Belgrade wouldn't talk to us, but their cross-town rivals were only too happy to. Sure, they said, let's have a beer together, we'll tell you some stories, it'll be fun...

The Gravediggers of Partizan Belgrade – 'Fuck the football'
We'd been put in touch with Johnny, top boy with a branch
of the Grobari calling themselves Alcatraz. Not only did they
have a reputation for being among the more extreme (for
which read, psychotic) Partizan fans, but they also held
within their ranks some of the real old school Gravedigger
hooligans. We couldn't help but wonder if some of these
same men had been there during the Balkans conflict, if these
were lads who had seen action on the front lines.

Johnny himself was a thin, wiry guy in his early twenties
with glasses and a completely shaved head. If the first
thought that came into our minds was that he looked a little
like the pop singer Moby, the second was that he also clearly
knew a thing or two about trouble. You could see it in his
eyes, the way he watched us; the cocky Englishmen who
thought they knew the score; the West Ham and Man United
fans whose firms they used to look up to but who they left
behind years ago. He was sizing us up. And by his grin, his
eager eyes, the twitchy, fizzing, ready-to-go energy he was
giving off, you could tell he really didn't rate us too highly.

Johnny and his crew were having a party and we were
invited. Within minutes of arriving we were shitting ourselves.

Beforehand, we'd had a drink and a discussion as to how
we were going to handle the situation. The sunshine and
piazzas and gorgeous girls of Split seemed a lifetime away –
since we'd arrived in Belgrade everything had got a whole lot
more tense.

Maybe it was the lack of trust the Delije had shown in us –
but suddenly we weren't quite so comfortable with Johnny
and the Grobari boys. We were getting claustrophobic,
paranoid. Someone said the word 'trap'.

Someone else said the word 'bollocks'. Look, went the reasoning, the Grobari have got no argument with us. We go in there like we went into the Maksimir, or the Torcida HQ: with respect. They invited us to a party, for Christ's sake. They were being friendly.

And besides: how bad could it be? We'd come through some of the liveliest Britain had to offer – we'd been in the Isle of Dogs and Moss Side as it all went off around us, we'd kept our head down at Old Firm Derbies and worse; we'd just last week stood on the terraces with an army of The Bad Blue Boys. We reckoned we'd be alright with a beer and a chat with some Partizan fans.

The party was held at a restaurant owned by one of the older Gravediggers: and if it wasn't exactly the wildest, most debauched do we'd ever heard about, it was also not your average jolly boys get together. We'd eased any lingering nerves with a round of shots necked before we left the hotel; and Danny went into extreme charm mode from the moment we arrived, sticking out his hand and striding up to groups of drinking hooligans. 'Good to meet you boys, pleasure, nice one, how are you?' he grinned, working his way around the room, shaking hands, smiling, keeping steady eye contact. He received curt nods in reply.

A couple of the men there seemed like veterans. One with a greying beard and glasses was afforded particular respect. He looked like a twinkly old uncle; his name was Zare and, as it turned out, he was not exactly the kind of uncle you'd want to offer you a sit on his knee and a suck of his Werther's Original.

But we didn't know that yet. For the moment we were all being handed beers and Johnny was explaining what it meant to be a Gravedigger of Partizan Belgrade.

'For us football is life,' he said, in response to Danny's question. 'And we fight for the name of Partizan and Grobari. Do you understand me? Football is life for us. Every member of Alcatraz is hard, we don't have soft members and we don't have time for soft people.'

And when Johnny's firm fight, they don't mess about. 'When we have weapons we fight with weapons; when we don't have weapons we fight with no weapons,' he said. 'What weapons do we use? Everything. Anything. Like in the war. No rules. In Belgrade, there are no rules. It's a poor country, a crazy country. No rules. And every time we see them [Red Star] we fight.' He shrugged. 'It is no problem. Two, three, four o'clock in the morning? No problem. We fight every time we see each other.'

We were interrupted by a large silver tray on which were neatly chopped little lines of coke. We declined as politely as we could – and were asked that perhaps we'd like to see their guns instead? Guns? Sure, Peter said, cool...

Suddenly, everyone there had a gun. We couldn't tell if they were replica or the real thing, but they looked authentic enough for us not to want to take the chance. Stuffed into the waistbands of their jeans or kept nonchalantly in jacket pockets, they were all at once unholstered, cocked and waved around like we were all in *Reservoir Dogs*. They wanted Peter and Stan to film them with their guns and their coke. They kept their eyes on the camera, their faces uncovered. They checked the tape, made him do it again. They wanted to be sure they looked good. They didn't give a shit who might see the footage – they were the Alcatraz Grobari of Partizan Belgrade, and as far as they were concerned, that meant they were untouchable.

'We're not in fucking Kansas anymore, Toto,' muttered Stan, and we started to laugh. We were so far out of our depth it was ridiculous. What could we do? We stopped worrying and started to relax. After all – here we were, in the back room of a backstreet restaurant somewhere in Belgrade, sharing beers with one of the most violent firms in Europe, watching as they passed around lines of coke and posed for photos with their pistols. 'Welcome to Belgrade!' they shouted. And all at once everyone pointed their guns at us.

There was a moment of absolute silence. And then someone started to sing and they all dropped their hands and joined in. We breathed again.

The song was in honour of Zare and his alleged part in what has become Gravedigger legend. In 1988, two years before the riot at Maksimir and three years before the official start of the war, a summit was held in Belgrade between the Torcida of Split and the Grobari of Partizan. The story goes that Torcida sent their top boy Parangal to Serbia to talk about a joint assault on their common enemies at the Maksimir and the Marakana.

And at first, all went well. The Grobari bought Parangal a few drinks, exchanged some gifts, showed him a few sights. Including one sight in particular: the grave of Dragan Mance, the gifted Partizan striker who died in a car accident in 1985 aged just 22. 'Kiss the grave,' Parangal was told. He refused. 'Kiss the grave,' he was told again. He refused again.

What happened next ensured that, however intense the rivalry might get between the two Croatian or the two Serbian sides, things would always be a lot worse when Serbs and Croats faced off against each other.

The other men around us started chuckling as Johnny

told the story, leaning over towards us, his eyes bright, dancing. 'They were not so hospitable as us,' he said, 'they take him there and tell him to kiss the grave, and he say, "Oh, I don't want to." So they say, "okay then we're going to have some fun..."'

The 'fun' was the repeated rape of Parangal. According to some versions of the story he was raped right there in the graveyard; according to others right there and then repeatedly for two full days afterwards; according to another, right there, for two days afterwards... and most often with a broom handle.

'You know when you say to someone, "we're going to fuck you"?' said Johnny. 'We actually mean it. We. Fucked. Him.'

By this time Johnny had a wide grin on his face and everyone around us was laughing. Especially, we suddenly noticed, Zare. He licked his lips and waggled his eyebrows. 'Oh, we miss them,' laughed Johnny, 'especially our friend Zare here, he has a very strong erotic and sexual connection with them, especially their leaders...'

As everyone erupted again, we laughed too but we weren't exactly amused. More like terrified. Kidnap and rape weren't on our wish list of experiences in Serbia and Johnny and his crew were eyeballing us in a way that was, frankly, getting pretty uncomfortable.

Danny had one more question. The camera was still rolling and he wanted to know if, given all that, the Grobari would still relish a match against Hajduk Split. After everything that happened, he said. We held our breath.

'Sure,' grinned Johnny, 'yeah we would want that, with the Croatian clubs it would be good, because there'd be more tension.'

Better football too?

'Better football for sure,' he said, 'but you know what?' And he grinned again. 'Fuck the football. Fuck the football.'

Watching the Gravedigger crew get rowdier, comparing firearms and singing songs about raping their opponents, it seemed we'd come an awful long way since touching down in Split. Our journey had started in the beautiful seaside resort in the sunshine, eyeing girls who looked like supermodels and shooting the breeze with a firm so organized they ran their own bar. And we'd ended up here, in a backstreet restaurant in Belgrade in the dark, passing round cheap cocaine with a bunch of gun-packing hooligans who consider rape to be a valid – and amusing – way of expressing their club loyalty.

How did it come to this? We didn't want to hang about to find out. After war and guns and rape, we didn't want to know what came next. We were out of there. We were done with Croatia and Serbia.

CHAPTER THREE

POLAND

The Poles are hard. They've had to be. This is the country that defeated both fascism and communism. It's a place well used to violence, to kicking against authority. It's a place where the usual rules don't seem to apply.

And it's home to some of the most serious football firms anywhere in the world. Remember Britain in our 1980s hooligan heyday? That's a bit like how it is here now – only with better weapons, greater organization... and more blood. There are reckoned to be around 100 gangs and 50,000 hooligans having tear ups across this country. It is a cauldron of violence.

We had come to Poland to meet the top boys of this new breed of ultra-ruthless fanatic; and we were going to be shown just what it means to be a hooligan out here. Twenty years ago football fans signed up as footsoldiers for the anti-communist uprising... and we were going to see how today those ideals have been forgotten in favour of a simpler kind of hostility. We were going to experience it ourselves, become part of the beating, bloody heart of the mob on the terraces at the most explosive derby in Eastern Europe: part inferno, part all-out riot.

We were here to gain unprecedented access to the Polish underworld. We were going to meet tooled-up blokes in balaclavas in shady places straight out of snuff movies. We were going to taste pure, vicious hatred.

We were going to need a shitload of vodka.

Welcome to Poland.

Here's the first thing you need to know about Poland: Poland is cold. It's freezing. Scarves that keep out the chill on an FA Cup weekend in January don't cut it here. If you're going to handle Poland in the winter you had better wrap up warmer than you do for Upton Park.

If it was brass monkeys outside it wasn't much better inside. Polish trains don't do heating it seems. We travelled right across the country, 240 miles north of Warsaw and then back 180 miles south of the capital, turning blue in a locomotive icebox, counting the hours and watching our breath misting up the windows, our hands thrust into pockets or cupping duty free cigarettes for warmth. All except for Danny, who was smoking Gitanes. It was a new look he was trying, he said. He wanted to see if it gave him a sort of existential poet-philosopher vibe.

It was so cold we couldn't even be bothered taking the piss.

The end of the line lay in Krakow. Out of Dworzec Glowny train station and into a taxi and it was still freezing – and the driver wasn't about to do anything about it. Stan was all for kicking off at him, until he realized that the car was older than he was; that it was a miracle the engine even turned over; that the fare for the journey wouldn't get us through the door of a black cab back home, even if it would be toasty warm inside.

He asked the driver instead what team he followed.

There was silence.

'Football?' said Stan, leaning forward, 'you know, like Man United? Er, Real Madrid? Legia Warsaw? Yeah? Who do you support? Cracovia? Wisla Cracow?'

He just shook his head and kept his mouth shut. We couldn't work out if he didn't want to tell us because he couldn't understand us, because he couldn't be bothered with us, or whether it was because he'd learnt through bitter experience that shouting off about your allegiances to total strangers is not a smart move in this town. People get mugged here for their scarves. Some have got killed for their teams. And this weekend especially was no time to be taking chances. This was derby weekend in Krakow. Last time Wisla Cracow and Cracovia clashed, a 21-year-old Wisla fan died for his club. To the local crews, dying is no big deal.

As Tyca, the top boy with the Cracovia firm Anty Wisla put it: 'What is the truth? This guy wasn't walking innocently and suddenly a bunch of Cracovia supporters attacked him and stabbed him to death... he was with his guys as well. They attacked the Cracovia supporters' bus.' He shrugged. 'Here in Krakow people have been dying and they are dying. There is always a possibility that they will die.'

For this fixture, tensions in the city were high. Riots were predicted.

We checked in and went straight out. The old part of Krakow's a pretty town and has some cracking bars: none of us had been here before and we had a night off before our business with the local troublemakers... and we wanted to make the most of it.

Danny, however, wasn't happy from the start. He had goose bumps. 'This whole place is unknown to me,' he said, as we dropped our bags at the hotel and took off to see what was happening. In the early Krakow evening, as people made their way home from work, or else strolled out for a bite and a drink, there didn't seem much to be concerned about. There were no hooligans in the medieval Grand Square.

But Danny had the jitters nonetheless. 'I can feel it,' he said, shivering. 'This is going to be a rollercoaster. I've got to admit I'm a bit worried about who we're going to meet. Are they going to let us into their world? Or are they going to tell me in no uncertain terms where to go? And what happens if they do?'

The locals can be a bit tasty, admitted Peter, who among us had probably done the most research into the hoolies of this particular part of Europe. Yes, he said, he wasn't going to lie: there was a definite risk of running into serious trouble. Securing insurance for this leg of our tour, he admitted, had been a problem.

Danny stopped in his tracks. 'What? Well then can somebody please tell me why I've agreed to come here? Where's a bar? I need a little cheeky vodka. What's Polish for Dutch Courage? Anyone? No? Jesus...'

He stalked off, swearing. We looked at each other. At this stage, Danny didn't know the half of it. Peter had set us up with the very nastiest Poland had to offer. We were going places the insurance people, the police, even our local researchers all advised us not to. We were going in there alone, with no backup.

We were going in there precisely because they didn't

want us to. We were going in there because they told us not to. We'd come looking for trouble. And we were going to find it, too.

Stan shrugged. 'Vodka it is, then.'

By the time we'd got to Krakow we'd actually been in Poland nearly a week. We'd flown into the capital Warsaw and we'd swung by the northern city of Gdansk. But these places were preludes to the real action; they were warm-up bouts before the main event.

And the main event meant Krakow. The place they call the City of Knives.

Krakow operates outside the rules, its hooligans renegade even to other hooligans. The big firms in Warsaw and Poznan have agreed rules for their rucks, they arrange fights in locations away from the city centres, with specified numbers on each side and carefully defined guidelines on what weapons are and aren't allowed. They've been turning hooliganism into a kind of extreme sport, with its own set of standards.

Not so in Krakow. There are no rules here. Hatred and fear are the only standards that matter.

'Krakow is a specific city,' Tyca was to explain to us. 'We are divided here into block districts belonging either to Cracovia or Wisla. There are streets where if you go across, you are at the enemy's territory. You can go to the shop and you will meet your opponent. Even to the cinema. We can meet anywhere, anytime. That's why this city is so special. In Krakow we have a war 24 hours a day.'

And it's this attitude that makes the Krakow firms among the most feared and respected in Europe. In the run up to the 2006 World Cup they were ranked with the English thugs as the principal security threat in Germany. *The Times* even ran a piece with the headline 'Polish hooligan army to invade World Cup' in which they warned of a super hardcore of 12,000 dedicated hooligans out to take over Berlin.

Despite the massive police presence at the tournament, the Poles nonetheless took on the German fans – and in the unofficial hoolie world cup, quickly became known as the firm to beat. More so than the English, even – a point that was made crystal clear to us by three of the top boys from the Wisla Sharks firm.

'Everyone knows that hooliganism originates from England,' we were told. 'They are not our inspiration though. We live in two different worlds. Here, the situation is not the same as in England. Maybe that's why they can't show what they are able to, like in the old times... But we think we are better than they are. We are the best and we can confront anyone. There will be a time... Everyone will see what Polish hooliganism is like.'

And among the Poles themselves, there's little argument about which mobs currently enjoy the most brutal reputation. Between them, the two Krakow teams play host to the most fearsome outfits in the country.

We were here to meet the top men of both the main Krakow firms – the Sharks of Wisla Cracow and the Anty Wisla of Cracovia. Just talking with one mob could get you fingered by the police – or worse, marked out by the other crew. And we were going to get into the heart of them both, on their manors, according to their terms... As if that wasn't enough, we were also here to join them on the terraces of the Wisla stadium as they clashed for the Krakow derby, the game they call The Holy War, and one of the most explosive fixtures in world hooliganism. It was to rank up there with the most terrifying experiences of our lives.

We got through it with a lot of vodka and a lot of cigarettes. By the time we left Poland we were all 60 a day men – and Danny had abandoned the Gitanes and gone back to a more traditional smoke: he was chaining so many of the filterless French fags that he was in danger of losing his voice.

It had all started so differently. If Krakow was like going undercover in a war zone, Gdansk was more like a cultural tour of hooligan theory.

To try and understand what makes Polish hooligans the force they are today, we had to go back to the beginnings of trouble on the terraces, we had to seek out the firm who started it all. And in doing so, we uncovered a kind of potted history of post-war Polish protest, how tooled up boys in Lechia Gdansk scarves took on the Communist authorities… and won.

• • •

Lechia Gdansk – 'on the trees, instead of leaves we will hang Communists'
The industrial city of Gdansk lies in the north of Poland, on the shores of the Baltic Sea. It's the country's principal seaport and feels like it too – the tension between the human traffic passing through, the sailors on leave with money to spend, and the local populace – the dockers and shipbuilders struggling for work, the local youths with little to nothing in the way of local opportunities… it spills over into trouble most weekends. Gdansk is a hard town, a tough town. People here are well used to handling themselves.

After the USSR took control of Poland after the Second World

War, Gdansk became the major industrial centre of the new country, the so-called Communist People's Republic of Poland. Under Soviet rule the Polish people were denied free elections, free speech, free protest. Opposition to the official party line was outlawed, any dissenting voices severely punished: trials were staged, those who spoke out were imprisoned or executed. For some, it felt that the simple fact of being Polish could be enough to get you in trouble with the authorities.

All except in one respect. The Soviets couldn't control what happened on the football pitch. And the militia soon found they couldn't control what happened on the terraces. At Lechia Gdansk games, the Polish people found their voice again; their hooligans started a movement that would end in the overthrow of the government.

We spent a day in the city with Zbigniew Zalewski: an old school troublemaker of the political variety as well as the football kind, he's now something of an expert on the collapse of communism in Poland. He took us to the shipyard where in 1989, the Solidarity movement, led by former shipworker Lech Walesa, became the first democratic Polish political party since Hitler had invaded 50 years earlier, and would finally send the communists packing.

He also took us to the stadium of Lechia Gdansk. If the shipyards are recognized in the history books as the birthplace of Solidarity, what those books don't tell you is that it was on these terraces that Polish civil unrest first found its feet. And its fists.

'This stadium is a special place,' he explained, waving his arms around the blank terraces and concrete stands and explaining how in the 1980s the local firm became a focus and breeding ground for the underground resistance. 'Stadiums were full back then. Nowadays press and media praise 10 or 12,000 attendance. But then we could go to the second [division] league games and there were 25 or 30,000 people coming. At that time stadiums gave us the only possibility to gather together to demonstrate that we had something in common. And everyone in Poland believed the same.

'The regime ruled the country and we wanted to show the negation of the system. The stadium gave the opportunity for the groups to gather. They put up the banners, chanted the slogans. Our club is the only one that has the flag with a principal slogan: "on the trees, instead of leaves we will hang the communists". And we still put it up during the games. It became a motto for the people.'

The idea took hold. Within months what had started as a tight crew of Lechia fans mouthing off about the government, became a firm, a mob, a great mass of people gathering every week on the terraces and letting fly at the authorities. 'After the games a few thousand of the mob marched along the streets crying out club and anticommunist slogans,' said Zbigniew. 'The game made the situation easier. A mass of people could come out and protest against communism.'

They weren't just vocal either. As the militia tried to put a lid on the protests, the trouble soon escalated into violence.

'The militia was the armed force of the communist regime and they reacted as if they were allergic to us,' shrugged Zbigniew. 'The tension between the militia and the marching crowd would rise up to the point that it needed to be released. Stones were thrown from one side and the reply to it was water hose. Someone threw the flare and got the gas can in return. Then the gas can was thrown back.'

And then the two sides – the people and the authorities,

the protestors and the police – would crash into each other. Truncheons were met with sticks, tear gas with stones, water cannons and rubber bullets with fists and knives. And despite being hopelessly outgunned, the hooligans were rarely outfought. The riots would last through the afternoon and long into the night, isolated pockets of trouble continuing off and on until the next match, the next proper opportunity for a riot. Even as our firms were living out their 1980s glory days in weekend clashes in pubs and high streets across Britain – clashes that lasted an hour or two at most – in Gdansk the hooligans were fighting for something more fundamental. They were tearing it up for their right to vote, they were taking on the police in the name of their freedom.

Every week would see fans arrested, hospitalized, even killed as the militia came down hard on anyone suspected of anti-communist protest. Being caught wearing a football scarf was often enough to ensure a beating from the military police... and yet every week the numbers on the Lechia terraces increased, the trouble after the game became more potent. When Lech Walesa's Solidarity swept to power in 1989, the Lechia firm were right there with them.

'That's it,' nodded Zbigniew. 'For sure, the Lechia supporters had been watched by authorities. They didn't like this circle as it was a potential danger for the system. The stadium was the place where the group of supporters could meet up. And this group was enough to cause problems. The city of Gdansk had the biggest part in destroying communism. Lechia stadium was the place where anyone could come. Simply, this stadium was a significant place, a magic place for us. We call it the Bastion of Independence.'

THE REAL FOOTBALL FACTORIES

The Bastion of Independence. Sure beats the Reebok Stadium as a name. But if we left Zbigniew and Gdansk in reflective mood, wondering – and not for the first time on our round-the-world hoolie tour – how football violence can be a force for real political change, a quick reflection on the scene here since the collapse of communism was enough to bring us back to earth. If the firms spent the 80s fighting for the people, they've spent the time since fighting among themselves. Hooliganism has soared across the country... in both numbers and nastiness.

Every major team has its own firm, huge mobs hundreds-strong who live for their weekend tear-ups. The Teddy Boys and Tourists of Warsaw, the Young Freaks of Poznan and the Cannibals of Lodz have all acquired reputations across Europe for the viciousness of their outfits. But Krakow's got the naughtiest of the lot.

• • •

Our first night in Krakow was spent trying to drink through the jitteriness of what was to come. The place might have a reputation among those who know as a breeding ground for football violence, a city of knives, but it's also making a bit of a name for itself as a stag party town. Step off the postcard-pretty medieval square and take the right turns and you're in a world of vodka bars, discos, strip clubs... and with more English voices than you get in central London these days.

After a traditional Polish dinner of sausages and chips, we sat around a trestle table slick with spilled lager and started to amass a collection of shot glasses. Peter ran through the agenda.

'Tomorrow,' he said, 'we're going to meet the Anty Wisla. These are Cracovia's top boys and they are serious fuckers. They didn't want to play ball originally and it's taken a lot of negotiations to get them to talk, so please, let's not piss them off too much.'

Danny perked up. 'Sweet,' he said, 'so we're meeting the top men, yeah? The organ grinders and not the monkeys? What's the plan? In a bar? Or at the ground?'

Peter shifted a little uncomfortably. 'Ahh, um, not exactly,' he said. 'They're being a little bit secretive on that score... we'll know for sure tomorrow.'

The rest of the evening was spent downing shots and dodging pissed stag parties eager to get their pictures taken with the cockney geezer off the telly. Some of us don't remember too clearly events past about 2am; and some of us aren't sure whether to believe everything we've been told about our behaviour concerning Polish lapdancers. But one of us woke up with his arse covered in bruises.

We were lucky it was just bruises. This might be a party town for British stag tourists... but it's probably best not to get too pissed here. And definitely not near derby day. Wander into the wrong part of town, wear the wrong colours, and it could be the last thing you ever do.

Away from the neon lights and ancient architecture of the old town, Krakow's suburbs are a desert of housing estates, vast concrete blocks thrown up during the years of communist rule and now home to a population of young, angry, unemployed men.

Solidarity might have thrown off the shackles of communist dictatorship in 1989, but the bitter legacy of those years remains. Unemployment has spiralled – as many as one in three on these estates are out of work – and a failing economy has meant that if you're young and male and Polish, your prospects aren't exactly rosy. Some have directed their energies into a Polish hip hop movement, some have slipped into lives of casual, petty or violent crime... most have simply followed the crowd to the football ground.

Put simply: for most of the lads, there is nothing else to do here. There's no work to be had; there's no money to spend. Your team, your firm, your gang, gives you the only pride you're going to get.

The gangs rule the estates. And the estates are defined by their teams. Cracovia here, Wisla there. Muggings are not only a regular occurrence, they're almost expected: rival mobs make a point of targeting anyone they see in a club scarf, or wearing a club shirt – opposition colours are collected like trophies, like the little swastikas fighter pilots would paint on their planes to denote enemies taken down.

In the 18 months before our visit eight fans had been killed in clashes between the city's two firms – the last victim was a Wisla fan dragged from his car and stabbed to death by a Cracovia mob on derby day.

And while the rest of Poland has attempted to rein in the worst excesses of the hooligan firms – signing non-aggression pacts between some clubs, declaring weapons to be off-limits, even abandoning trouble at the matches altogether in favour of organized rucks in 'safe' places away from the city – the Krakow mobs have just got nastier. Even as the firms from Warsaw were laying down their weapons, they were tooling up here. Everyone has a knife.

The rivalry between Wisla and Cracovia is every bit as intense as anything Britain has to offer – and soaked through with fully 100 years of hatred. It goes beyond the mere accident of their sharing a city. Wisla have traditionally been the stronger side – winning the Polish League title 10 times to Cracovia's five – and have also enjoyed greater financial stability than their poorer rival across the city. But what really rankles Cracovia fans is Wisla's origins as a football club set up by the militia.

'Wisla is the police club and everyone knows that,' said Tyca. 'They don't want to admit it – but if John is a dickhead and he has changed his name to Paul, he is still a dickhead. That's where the hatred between Cracovia and Wisla supporters comes from. That's also where the name "dogs" comes from. Wisla supporters are called dogs – the same name as for the policemen. We are dog hunters. Simple. We hate them like we hate the police.'

It was that hatred which gave the Cracovia firm their name. While most hooligan outfits define themselves by what they believe, by the image they want to project – think of the Yid Army, the Inter City Firm, the Suicide Squad, all those impressively-titled crews – the Cracovia mob identify themselves not through what they are but through what they aren't. They are the Anty Wisla.

And the night after whatever happened with the vodka and the lapdancers, we were supposed to be delving into the heart of this hatred.

Peter hadn't been lying: we did have a meeting with Cracovia's top boys. But what he hadn't told us was that it was to be on their terms, and according to exact instructions. We were to meet them in a petrol station in an area on the edge of the city, just after 11pm. We would then be directed to another location where the interview could take place. We were to leave our mobile phones at the hotel. And any funny business, he was told, would go badly for us.

If they were planning to leave us in shallow graves, they couldn't have gone about it any more thoroughly. And, like proper mugs, we just played along. What else could we do?

Peter insisted it was all cool – it turned out that the Cracovia firm had clashed with the police a couple of weeks before and had technically been banned from the forthcoming derby by the Polish FA. It had put them a little bit on edge, he said, but the good news was that the ban had just been lifted. The Anty Wisla were going to get their seat allocation for the derby after all. And that meant they would get their riot and therefore were bound to be in a good mood.

'So it's alright,' he grinned, as he drove the hire car through the dark Krakow streets in the rain, 'they're just being a bit... cautious. They don't know us from Adam, right? We could be anyone. Foreign police. We could be, you know, Interpol. They've got to be careful of us.'

'And what if they do think we're Interpol?' asked Stan.

'Well then we're fucked,' he replied cheerfully. 'Ah, here we go.' He pulled into a desolate looking garage forecourt and peered out of the windscreen. 'Probably best if we all wait outside the car,' he said, 'they might want to see how many of us there are.'

Danny looked at him incredulously, before checking on how many Gitanes he had left. He lit one, and immediately took another out ready to light straight after. He was going to need every one of them.

Eventually a car pulled up. We stood around smoking and stamping our feet, trying to work up some warmth, trying not to look like policemen, trying not to look like we were shitting ourselves, while Peter had a word with the driver.

'They want us to follow them,' he said, 'we're going to a, well...' he glanced apologetically at Danny. 'They're taking us to a tunnel.'

'We're going to a tunnel,' he said. 'Fucking great.'

The Anty Wisla of Cracovia – 'Yes, there is a possibility that you will die'

We followed the car for at least half an hour through streets that grew more and more deserted until even the estates looked abandoned and it seemed the headlights of our two vehicles were the only light for miles around. And then they turned off the road altogether, rolled to a stop and directed their lights back towards an underpass. Sure enough, there was a tunnel. It was strewn in bricks, crumbling concrete, empty cans and decorated with graffiti and some major stains that looked nastily like blood. It was the sort of place you really wouldn't want to stay long in. It was the sort of place you'd film a snuff movie.

Out here, no one would hear us scream.

If our nerves had been stretched before, they were close to breaking point now. Danny sparked another cigarette. 'This is the tunnel then,' he said, drawing hard and then grimacing. 'The undisclosed fucking tunnel. Looks like we might have a bit of joy here. I've got to say I am a bit apprehensive – I don't know how they're going to react to me.' He looked at his fag. 'For a start I might look a bit of a prick with a Gitanes in my hand. Knew I should have had a fucking Benson.'

We got out of the car. Stan turned the camera on, Peter checked his watch, Danny turned up his collars, took a deep breath, and we all started walking. At the mouth of the tunnel, silhouetted against the headlights, we could see four figures, their breath freezing in clouds around them. 'Right,' muttered Danny. 'This is about composure and trust. It's about respect. Here we go then, let's fucking have it...'

He walked up to the nearest man and stuck his hand out. 'Alright,' he said, 'nice to meet – hang on son. Is that West Ham you're wearing?'

Sure enough, although all four of the Anty Wisla crew were bundled up in black jackets and black jeans, one of them had a Hammers baseball cap on. 'You fucking beauty!' said Danny, grabbing his collar and kissing him full on the head. 'Look at this! West Ham till I die!'

The boy with the baseball cap flinched as Danny snatched his cap and tried to ruffle his hair and two of the other crew instinctively reached inside their pockets. Stan and Peter exchanged a look and we got ready to run, until the fourth man – and the only one of them making no attempt to hide his face – cracked a broad grin.

'I'm Tyca,' he said. 'Welcome.'

Tyca is who we had come to meet. He's been active in the more extreme end of Cracovia football club for 27 years and he's got the scars to prove it. Standing over six feet tall and built like a wrestler, with shaved head and a stubbly goatee, he is the closest thing the Anty Wisla has to a living God; a true terrace legend, he's followed the club all his life and dragged his firm up from a small group of supporters to one of Poland's elite hooligan organizations.

He's also got that easy confidence that only men used to dealing in extreme violence seem to have. He didn't care about covering up his face for the cameras, or exaggerating past victories, or, really, what we thought of him at all. He was secure in the knowledge that whenever he wanted the interview to end, it ended. We were here on his terms. And although he never said it, we all knew that the same went for us. We were in his tunnel; we were at his mercy. We were his entertainment for the evening – nothing more.

Right now though, Danny was amusing him, so that was good. And first of all, he wanted to explain the origins of his firm.

'They call us "outsiders",' he said. 'I think it comes from the time when Cracovia was in the third division for 20 years. We didn't have any contact with other clubs from the first league, which means we missed meeting the hooligans who were at the top clubs. So the only time we could meet these guys was at the international games.' He grinned. 'And we showed at the international games that we could do a lot, while all the other teams started to unify and had these strange pacts and agreements. We weren't interested in that at all. We always wanted to go to a game and fight. And the result is that most of the clubs hated us because we broke all the non-aggression pacts.'

It was Tyca's contempt for any peace settlements between rival firms – as well as a burning desire to make his crew stand out from the rest – that saw him drive Anty Wisla to the top of the heap, even as the team improved on the pitch.

'In the beginning, Anty Wisla consisted of 53 people,' he said. 'There were 53 people in our circle who set up it all. We had 53 scarves and nobody could get into our firm by chance. That's how it started.

'We took over the style and names from England very quickly. We learned very fast. And we were different from the others. Guys from Gdansk, Poznan and Warsaw used to wear these bright yellow or orange tracksuits: it was a fashion in Poland that everyone used to wear tracksuits... but Cracovia guys wore Dr Martens and Levis 501. We were completely different. We were the first ones to come to the stadium all in black, in balaclavas. I remember, we marched in all in black, put balaclavas on and rushed into the rival supporters' sector. We caused a big panic on the stands.'

'So would you say you were inspired by the English then?' asked Danny.

'We would like to say to the English that they showed us everything. The beginning of hooliganism, everything that they've started. And as we are good pupils I guess, we've learned a lot from them and we know a lot now.' Tyca grinned, showing the gaps in his teeth. 'Maybe we know more.'

'More' by Tyca's definitions, means more extreme. He doesn't run Anty Wisla like a supporters club, or a glorified drinking society, or even like a big nasty bunch of mates who like to have a ruck at the weekend... he runs it like a criminal gang. Which, in a sense, is exactly what they are. Most of his firm don't have anything else in their lives; no jobs, no prospects, no thoughts of a future beyond the football season. Their world consists of the estates, the football stadium and whatever patches of ground like this they've claimed for themselves.

'In Krakow, these last 10 years belonged to Cracovia. We rule here,' he said.

He jabbed a finger at Danny. 'Listen, a good firm is prepared for anything, everyday. Especially in Krakow. Every day my firm is prepared for it. And most of the guys who fight know that they can be hurt, stabbed. They know that they can get a blow in the head like me. Almost everyone has got a wound.

'Every hooligan signs up for fights automatically. He has to realize that he can be hurt. Sometimes very seriously. Here, in Krakow, we've been using the knives for a long time. We just do that and that's it. And yes, there is a possibility that you will die.'

He held Danny's gaze. And Danny, to be fair, didn't back down. Or not straight away, anyhow. He asked him if he enjoyed fighting, if he got a buzz out of cutting someone up, kicking them to the floor, laying them out cold.

Tyca didn't smile. He simply nodded. 'It's an incredible rush of adrenaline,' he said, deadly serious. 'You don't think about anything. You don't feel anything. It's... it's something unbelievable. It's a great feeling. You could compare it to a drug. You can be addicted to it. And when it starts... you see the opponent and suddenly that's it. Everything switches off. You act as if you are in a kind of spacesuit and you have earphones on. You can't hear anything and the only thing you see is your enemy in front of you.

'It's a great feeling... you should try it sometime. If you try it once, you'll like it.'

And then suddenly that was it. Tyca yawned, he'd had enough. 'This is over now,' he said, and stared directly at Stan, who nodded dumbly until he realized what he meant and turned the camera off. 'Krakow town, your hotel,' said Tyca, 'it's that way,' and he pointed behind us.

We turned around, picked our way back through the tunnel to the car with our hearts hammering and the hairs on our neck standing up... and got the hell out of there.

The silence in the car as we drove back to civilization was eventually broken by Peter. 'So, that went well,' he said. Nobody answered, except Danny, who swore at him. 'Well we're all still alive aren't we?' he said. 'And tomorrow night we're meeting the Wisla Sharks. And, I, er, well, we're not quite sure exactly where yet...'

The Wisla Sharks – 'Here, if there is a war, there is a total war'
The following night was the evening before the big game: the 100th anniversary of the Krakow derby and the whole city was on red alert. Throughout the day there had been incidents and accidents – boys getting jumped for their scarves, running battles on the estates, at least one minor riot that spilled out of a bar and into the old town. There had been a handful of hospitalizations, a couple of arrests. By sundown the police were out in force and even the tourists looked jumpy. The place was primed to go off.

We weren't to be found with the tourists or the police. As the freezing night set in we were once again in the hire car, passing around a bottle of vodka and blowing on our hands to keep warm. Here we were: different night, different firm, same deal. The Wisla Sharks wanted to see us... but, like the Anty Wisla, it was to be on their terms, by their rules. We'd been left directions to another deserted spot on the edge of the city. It seemed the way the hooligan organizations did things in Poland was designed to be as intimidating as possible.

If we were shivering we couldn't tell whether it was from the cold or from nerves. After surviving one snuff movie-type experience, it felt a bit like we were pushing our luck to be driving straight into another.

And we were headed into the middle of nowhere. The directions Peter had were precise enough, but they ended with us right out of town and down a scrubby back road on some derelict land. The nearest buildings were a couple of half-demolished factories, windows gaping, all the glass long since smashed. Stan swore he heard a wolf howl.

Danny took another pull at the bottle. 'What do you reckon,' he asked, 'should I keep this up my sleeve, you know, just in case?'

Stan was about to tell him not to be so stupid as even think about trying it on with these boys, when the look on Danny's face stopped him. He might have a bit of front about him – but right then he was as scared as the rest of us.

'I'm joking man,' he said, 'why would I do that? Come on, one more shot and then let's have it.' He handed the bottle to Peter. 'I gotta hold my hands up,' he said, 'my popper is flapping a little bit. I am not a mug and my popper is flapping.'

Suddenly a set of headlights came on – illuminating three figures standing by a wall. All wore balaclavas and zipped up coats; none of them spoke. They looked terrifying. The whole scene was straight out of a horror flick.

'Fucking hell man. Jesus fucking Christ,' said Danny. 'This is naughty, this is fucking naughty...'

Stan turned the camera on and not for the first or last time on this trip, we tried to forget our terror and do what we'd come for. We walked over to the boys, Danny with his familiar open-armed approach, doing his full-on charm thing again. 'Pleasure to meet you, man, pleasure,' he said, shaking each of their hands. 'I don't know man. I don't know where the fuck I am. But I'm like... I love it man. I love this. This is fucking great. You couldn't build a set like this.'

One of them nodded. And then Danny did something mad. 'Can I just say first of all, maybe I'm a bit arrogant, but I wanna ask you about *The Football Factory*, the movie,' he said. 'Be honest with me. Be brutal. What did you make of that movie?'

Stan almost dropped the camera. There was a time and a place for doing the film star bit, for working the fans. In the middle of the night in shallow grave territory on the edge of Krakow with three knife-wielding hooligans in balaclavas was not it.

'It's shit,' said one of them.

'Yeah, you're probably right,' he replied cheerfully. 'So if you're not inspired by my work, are you inspired by the firms in England from the past, maybe?'

Weirdly – or brilliantly – it did the trick. All three laughed. One of them said something about another football film, about how American actors struggle with the genre a bit. How they look more like hooligans than hobbits.

'Everyone knows that hooliganism originates from England,' said the guy in the middle, the main man. 'It all started over there. They are not our inspiration though.'

'It works both ways,' said Danny. 'I would say that for the firms in England, you Polish, you have a lot of respect from us. We know that if the English firms are gonna go into a battle with the Polish, we know that you don't fuck about. You know, you rank highly. Do you like... how do you feel about fighting English firms? Is it a big moment for you?'

He shrugged. 'Sure, because English hooligans are still known in the whole world, even if they are not very good recently. But everything has moved forward. Before, hooliganism was based on going to games, drinking a couple of beers... Alcohol went to your head and that was it. It's completely different now.

'In 1999 in Saski Park in Warsaw we fought against the

English and we could see there is a difference between us. They arrived with beers, spontaneously. We defeated them because the Polish were very well organized. And even recently: Poland played against England. Our firms went to England. We wanted to fight against you guys, in a pub. You didn't want to. You barricaded the door and didn't want to go out.'

Peter asked if they could tell us their names – just for the caption on the TV show, he said. They shook their heads. No names. 'It's enough for you to know we are Wisla Sharks,' said one of them. 'That's all.'

'Course it is,' said Danny, 'you don't want to go shouting your name about, do you? Course not! You've got the Old Bill to think about. And what about tomorrow? The derby. Is it the biggest game in Poland? Are you ready for it?'

All three nodded. 'It is the most important day in our lives,' said the main man. 'There is a hate we were born with, that has been passed from father to son. Tomorrow, we express it.

'The situation is different from England. In Poland it wouldn't be possible to see people walking along the street wearing shirts of different clubs. I experienced it in England: three men in Manchester colours and two in Arsenal and they were talking and laughing with each other. There is no way you could see anything like this in Poland. Here, if there is a war, there is a total war. We fight however we can and whenever we can.'

For the Sharks, he explained, it's about more than football support, more than fighting even. It's their whole life. Like their enemies across the terraces, they came from a background of estates and unemployment. Like them their weekend fix of football and violence provided the only distraction from the stifling dullness of their normal lives... but, unlike Tyca's mob, this lot seemed a bit more disciplined, organized.

'In Poland a hooligan's lifestyle has got only one direction,' he said. 'You have to be strong. We do lots of training, gym and martial arts. You can't drink. The lifestyle is more like a sportsman than a fan.

'Our aim is to be the best, isn't it? If you have a certain goal in your life you have to sacrifice some things. We shouldn't drink alcohol and smoke because all this stuff makes us weak. We have to do everything to be the best. We have to exercise, exercise and once more... exercise.

'When we go to the stadium we are not the type of people who would blow the trumpet and wave the flag. We are brought up to be tough and we want to prove it.'

If the Anty Wisla had convinced us that their passion meant they were unafraid to go that extra mile for their firm, to step outside whatever rules other crews lived by, their deadliest rivals were no different.

'In Krakow weapons are used every day,' they said. 'The knife in the pocket is our daily bread. We'll use anything from knives to bats, from kitchen knives to farmer's tools. Even Molotov cocktails. Also there are guns. On several occasions, live ammunition has been used.

'That's the reason why the whole of Poland hates us. Everybody is afraid of us. Our rivals come to Krakow only when they know we are out of town or they are sure they are going to get a police escort. Otherwise they fear us.'

Suddenly a mobile phone rang. We all jumped – against the eerie atmosphere of the place, the surrounding pitch black and weird two-dimensional illumination the headlights gave, the shadows, the cold and the guttural accents and voices muffled by balaclavas, the familiar sound of a Nokia ringtone was just about the strangest thing of all.

One of the Sharks ducked away to answer it.

Danny asked the remaining two if they had ever been on the wrong side of a beating themselves.

'Of course. Sometimes several times throughout the day. That's our life. You go out to the shop and you can get attacked. Krakow is divided. Here, you can always come across someone you can have a fight with or you can meet someone who is trying to hunt you down.' He held out his hand – his little finger was missing and a crooked scar ran along the inside of his forearm from elbow to wrist. 'I got the knife in my hand several times that was aimed into my belly,' he said.

The man on the phone returned and made a gesture to the other two, the unmistakable finger drawn across the throat, the universal signal for execution.

'The interview's over,' said the man in the middle. He leaned forward. 'But don't worry. We have a surprise for you.'

Fuck… we instinctively backed off, towards the car. That sign, the finger across the throat: out here we wouldn't stand a chance. We wouldn't be found for days, weeks, months. Nobody knew we were here. We might never be found…

'Now then lads,' began Peter, but he was cut off.

'Some tickets have come up for tomorrow's game,' said the main man. 'It seems some of our boys had a bit of trouble tonight. If you like, you can come to the Krakow derby as guests of Wisla Ultras. Don't worry, we'll look after you good…'

'Tickets,' breathed Stan. 'They're giving us tickets. Fuck me. I think I've wet myself.'

• • •

Wisla Cracow v Cracovia – The Holy War

The next morning and Krakow was suffocating. The streets around the old square and the football stadium were thick with riot police in combat gear and balaclavas, truncheons and shields. From our hotel we watched as squads jogged towards the ground in formation – flanked by vans, armoured vehicles, dog handlers and their great, vicious, slavering Alsatians.

Also on the street were the fans, no longer hiding their colours: they were worn defiantly, though faces were almost uniformly covered. Those who didn't have balaclavas wore their scarves wrapped over their mouths and noses, with baseball caps low over the eyes. They stood in gangs of four, six, twelve. Nobody was drinking. Nobody was laughing. When they burst into song they weren't songs of support: they were songs of hate, they were challenges.

The whole place was itchy with the prospect of violence. There was no question of it not going off – it was just a matter of when, and how badly.

But this is why we were here. This is what we'd come for. All the tension and the build-up, the talk and the tales... it all ended here. This game of football, this meeting of deadly rivals across a city – this was what it was all about. This was Krakow's Holy War.

As we filed out of the hotel and walked in silence through the knots of fans and ranks of policemen all of our senses were heightened, everything on high alert. Stan was shivering uncontrollably; the bitter air smelt of burning.

Things were even more intense at the ground. Police were everywhere, their dogs snapping and sniffing as we tried to pass through. Riot vans littered the place like abandoned toy cars and at regular distances mobile water cannons were set up. The policemen manning them scanned the crowds like guards on the watchtowers of PoW camps.

The rival fans were kept apart but both sets were not averse to squaring up to the police: all around the place mini-confrontations were happening – non-physical at this stage, but loaded with intent. Suddenly we saw the unmistakable bulk of Tyca, head to toe in black and with a hood pulled up over his shaved head, nose to nose with a policeman, his eyes fixed on him, mouthing a steady stream of quiet, vicious abuse into the copper's face. They couldn't have been more than a few inches apart. Tyca's hands were in his pockets, the policeman's were on his gun.

We ducked away sharpish. We weren't sure if Tyca's mob knew we were coming to the match at all – but we definitely didn't want them knowing we were here as guests of the Wisla Ultras.

Our Ultras hosts were keen to stress that they are not hooligans. 'We are responsible for the performance inside the stadium,' they told us, 'banners, flares, choreography. And burning.'

Burning?

It seems that at half-time in the match the Ultras were to put on a display guaranteed to wind up the opposition fans as much as possible – all those Cracovia scarves, hats, shirts that the Sharks had spent months 'collecting' from their rivals were to be hung on the terrace fences, doused in petrol and set alight.

That was why they mugged each other for their scarves here. That's why people got beaten, stabbed, killed for their colours. So they could torch their own scarves in front of them. It was literally a case of adding insult to injury.

We slipped into Sektor A with the Wisla Ultras and surrendered ourselves to the mob. Our hosts had given us scarves and they motioned to us that we should cover our faces; given that we'd already seen Tyca once, we didn't need telling twice.

Around us were hemmed 5,000 of the Wisla faithful shouting themselves hoarse – all their energy directed across the pitch to the away stand. We could see the Cracovia firm packed in there, buzzing against the massive steel fencing like angry wasps.

In the moments before kick off the air grew thicker, the atmosphere more stifling: it got difficult to breathe, it felt like the big inhalation before the scream. Thousands of flares were lit, a massive roar went up... and in the surge we rushed forward with the rest of the crowd, shouting along even though we had no idea what we were saying.

The noise didn't let up once the game kicked off. Our eyes watering from the flares and our throats hoarse from shouting it was all we could do to try to look as excited as everyone around us. The choreographers were leading the singing, keeping everyone whipped up into a frenzy, ensuring the volume, the fervour, did not let up for a second.

On the pitch the game was going Wisla's way but to be honest it was impossible to pay much attention. All the action was happening in the stands.

'Keep an eye over there,' shouted Danny, pointing to the away stands, 'they mean business, they're not going to stay in there too long'. Suddenly there was a louder roar, a massive surge, a jolt like electricity through the stand. Wisla had scored and everything went mental. The Ultras were jumping and running and shoving and being shoved in every direction – the momentum carried Stan one way and Danny the other until both were lost in the mess of jubilant fans.

By the time we got ourselves together enough to regroup, Wisla scored again – and once more we were hurtled in opposite directions. Danny was kissing a scarf with a skinhead and Stan was shouting at a skinny, nasty seeming guy who looked a bit like Gollum: '2-0 in half an hour! They've only gone two fucking up!' Gollum scowled and turned away.

Down at the other end, the Cracovia firm were not so happy. Their silence was ominous: they stood in files, staring with loathing at the home fans. And then suddenly, seemingly out of nowhere and as one, they charged. Nearly a thousand of them smashed into the fence, completely wrong-footing the riot police who were waiting pitch-side.

'Look!' pointed Danny, 'the Sharks!'

The reason behind the sudden change in mood became clear – while all the attention had been focused on the Ultras in our section, the Sharks mob had quietly been massing in the stand next to the Cracovia firm: now some of them had set light to Cracovia shirts and were throwing them over the fences. The reaction was immediate – and incredible. The Anty Wisla went crazy, hurling themselves at the barricades, throwing themselves at the fences. As the police raced between them, shields above their heads and batons swinging, the Sharks laughed. This was just the start of their taunting.

At half-time the real trouble began. The players were barely off the pitch before the tension was cranked up even further and the Wisla Ultras delivered the ultimate act of provocation. All around us boys were rushing down to the pitchside fences and flinging Cracovia scarves, shirts, flags on to them, the spoils of months of muggings, thefts, rucks and hospitalizations. A couple of the choreographers were on hand with cans of petrol and right behind them were the boys with the matches. Twisted firestarters.

Whoosh! The whole fence went up in a curtain of flame. There must have been 500 scarves up there – and that had meant 500 whacks to the head, 500 Cracovia fans taken down, laid out, humiliated. And now they were pressing home that humiliation, they were putting it right in their faces. Stealing your colours and then burning it in front of you... for the average Polish hooligan insults don't get much worse than that.

The heat was incredible, the acrid smoke making it difficult to breathe. Stan was doubled up coughing, Danny was shaking his head and swearing at the top of his voice. We hadn't seen Peter since kick off – he was supposed to be filming all this from pitchside. Christ knows how it looked from down there. From where we were the mad light from the flames and the flares turned everything red; it made the stadium look like a war zone, like a missile had gone off, like hell.

For the Cracovia hooligans, it was too much. If we thought they were angry before, now they went nuclear. Seats were being ripped up and launched over the fence towards the Wisla crew, or down the stand at the police. Impromptu weapons seemed to appear from nowhere, flagpoles and sticks used like spears; stones, bricks, anything they could get their hands on was picked up and hurled. Charge after charge was led against the fence, wave after wave of Cracovia hooligans ramming against the barriers. When it began to look like it might give way, when the seats and bricks and flagpoles were joined in the air by knives, the police finally mounted a counter charge.

The two sides clashed amid roars from around the stadium and even as the second half got underway, all attention was on the battle for the terraces: the Anty Wisla held the high ground, throwing down anything they could find on to the coppers; and the police responded with tear gas. It took most of the second half and a lot of smashed up seats, injured coppers and laid out hooligans before the situation was under control again. The match ended 3-0 to Wisla on the pitch – and it looked like the Cracovia firm had taken a pasting off it too.

We took our chance while there was a lull and slipped away. Even as we hurried back to the hotel, our scarves now hidden under our jackets, people were beginning to mass on the streets again, crowds of jubilant Wisla fans; knots of furious, ashamed Cracovia boys. There was yet more police – it felt like every policeman in Poland was here – and the water cannons were already seeing some action. The roads were slick: as the temperature dropped they would freeze, the whole place would become like an ice rink... meaning more broken limbs, more cracked heads.

The trouble wasn't over yet. Vengeance was in the air and the firms could smell blood. We didn't want to hang around any longer. We'd seen too much of the City of Knives already. And we definitely didn't want to bump into Tyca. We were gone.

CHAPTER FOUR

HOLLAND

Holland – the most liberal country in Europe. A nation of chilled, easygoing geezers in funny orange wigs and wooden clogs, a place where the weed is legal and the working girls advertise themselves in shop windows. The home of good lagers, techno music and Johann Cruyff.

Oh yeah – and shootings, stabbings, bombings. Riots. Arson. Murder. There is a hidden Holland behind the stoned smiles and the stag dos, a place of intolerance and violence. And that's what we were really here for. We hadn't come to the Netherlands just to sample the funny cigarettes and the good time girls: we'd come to see a side of the country that has more in common with Baghdad than it does Jolly Boys' outings.

Nobody talks about Total Football where we were going. They talk about Total War.

We touched down in Schiphol with smiles on our faces and I swear as the plane bumped along the tarmac Stan was literally rubbing his hands together in anticipation. After a couple of weeks of high tension and feeling well out of our depth among tower blocks and back alleys in former communist states, it seemed like, finally, we were back in something like home territory. We all knew Holland; we'd all been here before.

And we'd all been looking forward to coming back: on paper it seemed one of the standout destinations on our round-the-hooligan-world trip. And not for anything to do with hooligans, either. 'Sex, drugs and clogs,' was how Danny described the home of van Gogh and Anne Frank. 'Larging it in the red light district or sitting outside some coffee shop smoking a great big fat spliff.'

But Europe's most liberal capital held something else in store for us.

It held the notorious F-Side firm of Ajax Amsterdam, for a start – and a man in shades and a Burberry baseball cap who would produce a stick of dynamite like he was going to blow up a safe or something. An actual stick of dynamite.

'I'm not a murderer,' he would tell us, calm as you like. 'Not yet. But if you touch one of my friends I'll fucking kill you.'

And, like Stan said: that's not the kind of shit you expect to hear from a man with a stick of TNT in his hand. (Peter asked him what he would expect. After thinking about it, Stan nodded. 'Run like fuck,' was his answer.)

This same firm was responsible for crossing that invisible hooligan line – they turned their attention to taking out footballers. In 2004, shortly before he signed for Arsenal, Robin van Persie was attacked by Ajax hooligans during a reserve game between the Amsterdam club and their hated Rotterdam rivals Feyenoord. As 250 members of the F-Side invaded the pitch, the players ran for their lives – van

Persie didn't run fast enough. He sustained severe head and neck injuries as well as bruised ribs and only escaped worse when Ajax youth team coach Marco van Basten threw himself on top of the young striker. Van Basten was spared the wrath of the Ajax firm but other Feyenoord players who tried to help were beaten so badly they left the ground in ambulances.

'There was a friendly game, where the second teams were playing each other and suddenly it went off,' laughed our boy with the dynamite. 'You know personally I don't like attacking players but...'

'Shit happens,' said his friend, face hidden behind a ski mask.

'It was Van Persie so...'

'Shit happens,' he repeated.

'Shit happens,' he laughed again. 'Sorry... but Van Persie is a cockroach. He comes from Rotterdam. And we hate everybody who comes from there, we hate them all. There's only Amsterdam; there is nothing else.'

Sex, drugs and clogs. Nice idea, Danny.

• • •

First things first. Our researchers had been out here making contact with the top Dutch firms for a few months before we turned up: same as in all the countries we visited, there were boys behind the scenes setting it all up. Their work was vital: we wouldn't have got anywhere without them. Obviously you can't just go waltzing into these places and expect to talk to committed hooligans, convicted criminals, the kinds of blokes who might be packing blades, even guns (even, as it turns out, sticks of dynamite). Try it and see how far you get – as likely as not it'll be about as far as A&E.

Despite the temptations of late-night Amsterdam, we weren't tourists, we weren't spectators: we were here to make a TV series. We were here to find out about the world football hooligan scene, to see how it has thrived, grown and evolved even as our own firms have been pushed underground... but we were also here to do a job. We were professionals, right?

'Right,' said Stan as we walked through the massive shopping precinct that is Schiphol airport, past the tulip stalls and the clog merchants and the people selling Sunflowers tea towels; 'Right,' he repeated, his eyes following a pack of girls here on a hen do, skirts barely over their arses, all bare arms and legs and angel wings and devil horns, tottering and giggling and passing around duty free vodka... 'Right, we're professionals. We're here to do a job.'

Everyone stopped – and then burst out laughing.

'Nice one Stan,' said someone. 'Now let's go get battered.'

As usual, the researchers had done their job brilliantly. Peter had our itinerary and, if it was packed, it was also pretty comprehensive. We were going to be visiting four cities while in the Netherlands – Amsterdam, Rotterdam, Den Haag and Utrecht – and in each of them had planned to meet the most hardcore firms in Dutch football.

In the capital we were going to meet the F-Side of Ajax; before moving to Rotterdam the very next day to take our place on the terraces with the Feyenoord crew for the explosive Feyenoord v Ajax match. The game is known as one of the most passionate – and violent – fixtures in Europe and we were going to be right in there among it. After that, it was back in the hire car to Den Haag, home to the Dutch Parliament and a firm called the Northside with a reputation for viciousness that for many far outstrips their team's abilities on the pitch. Finally, we were headed for Utrecht and the veterans of the Bunnikside... as well as the next generation of thugs promising to take Dutch football violence well into the future.

We were kind of into the swing of things now. Or so we thought. We had got used to meeting first one firm and then the other, had got the hang of dealing with deadly rivals. As long as you showed them equal respect, we figured, they'll be cool. As long as you don't take the piss. And then of course, we had our team out here laying the groundwork for us, making the contacts, setting up the meetings, sorting it all out. And this was Holland, anyway. The most laid-back country outside of the Caribbean. What could go wrong?

Plenty, as it turned out. Holland may have felt like a cakewalk as we strolled through Schiphol eyeing up the skirt and anticipating the evening out – but it wasn't to pan out that way. We weren't as smart as we thought: or the Dutch were a little bit more feisty than we anticipated. Or a bit of both.

Either way, things were going to go a little bit off-script. And we were going to end up moving on a whole lot quicker than we'd planned.

• • •

Peter, the director, wanted to set up Danny's initial shots, his introduction to Holland, while walking through the crowds around the Red Light District and Dam Square. Bustling, cosmopolitan, thriving, modern – that was the idea. Somewhere your average man in the street would feel safe; somewhere light and bright and open, somewhere you'd never guess bred viciousness and hatred. And that's exactly how it felt too. It didn't feel like we were on the front line, like we were heading into the dark heart of European hooliganism. It felt like... we were in Amsterdam. We soon got into it.

'We should do a piece outside a coffee shop,' said Danny, pointing at a sign which read: Bulldog. 'Sweet as. Seriously. Fuck's sake boys. While we're here.' He sat down and caught a passing waiter. 'Hello mate, can we see the, ah, menu please?'

Peter looked at his watch and shrugged. We were due a break anyway.

A couple of hours later and we were pissing ourselves. Stan was struggling to skin up and Peter was almost crying into his drink. Danny had repeated the same couple of lines to the camera five times, fluffing a different word each time, and some of the locals were getting on his case, taking the piss. Danny was pretending to get narked, but he was loving it really, loving the attention.

'No I'm not mad, I'm not going mad sweetheart,' he scowled at one passing girl, 'I'm fucking working man.' He accepted the spliff off Stan and sat back. 'I'm working.

'Admittedly,' he laughed, 'I'm not working very hard right now. But I think, you know, you've got to try everything once. It's just fucking paradise for me, this gaff's absolute paradise. Can't understand why anyone would want to swing a punch. You know, I thought it'd be just chilled out, everyone stoned, cuddling each other all sharing a burger...

'What's that mate?' And he was off, deep in conversation with a surprised German on the next table. Nobody was sure what language either of them were speaking ('Sprechen-sie what? Dead fucking right, son!') and each new sentence set us howling again.

Okay, so it wasn't that funny, on reflection. But, to be fair, we were mashed.

Danny might have been a little under the loved-up influence of the finest Holland had to offer, but he did have a point. Why would anyone want to swing a punch in this town?

Guess what? It's all thanks to the English.

In 1974 Dutch football was the envy of the world. Cruyff, Johan Neeskens and national coach Rinus Michels were redefining the way the game was played – in the World Cup that year their 'total football' philosophy would see them beat both Brazil and Argentina on their way to the final… and go on to score against the Germans before their opponents had even had a touch of the ball. Back home, however, something just as significant happened.

On 29 May 1974, Feyenoord of Rotterdam hosted Tottenham Hotspur in the second leg of the final of the UEFA Cup. The score was 2-2 after the first leg at White Hart Lane – and Spurs would end up losing on the night and 4-2 on aggregate. For many, however, the match itself was irrelevant. That night Spurs fans ran riot through Rotterdam both before and after the game: 70 fans were arrested and over 200 people were injured as the north Londoners stormed the city. The Dutch didn't know what hit them – they had no hooligan scene to speak of, and certainly no organized firms – and they were no match for the Spurs mob. Images of rioting Englishmen shocked Europe that night, but also sparked something in the Dutch youth.

Now known in Holland as 'the day Dutch football lost its innocence', 29 May 1974 is also recognized as the birth of Dutch football hooliganism. Within six months all the big teams had their own firms, or 'sides', named after the sections of the grounds most likely to kick off.

They never looked back.

And, perhaps as befits Dutch football's most successful club team, the Ajax firm – or F-Side – quickly became one of the most feared in the country.

And, just as soon as we'd slept off the effects of all that skunk, we were going to meet them.

The F-Side of Ajax – 'You have to fight for your life and you look around and it's totally war, totally chaos.'

If Amsterdam was the first time we'd felt anything like relaxed on this trip, Ajax's stadium, the Amsterdam Arena, was also the first properly modern stadium we'd visited. Although it's got a relatively modest capacity for a modern European footballing superpower – 56,000 – it's a beautiful thing nonetheless: just 10 years old and still got the shine on. It's the kind of place that suits a team known for their culture and elegance on the field, all glass and steel and a sliding roof. 'It don't touch Upton Park,' sniffed Danny, 'but it's got something about it.'

We were here to meet the F-Side. And if Ajax are known for their casually superior attitude on the football pitch, their firm has got something like the same reputation for their approach to violence. They work alone. They don't form alliances and they don't side up with anyone – not even for national games. As far as they're concerned, they're the top boys and everyone else can fuck off.

Some of the other firms think that's a touch arrogant of them. They don't care.

'We do things on our own,' they told us. 'We are not

Holland supporters. We don't want to fight together with Feyenoord or Den Haag or somewhere. We hate everybody, we want to fuck everybody, you know? And they don't fucking like it. Everybody hates Amsterdam because we are the best.'

We had been told by our researchers that the F-Side would be happy to meet us – provided we play by their rules. No names and nothing that could give their identities away. Cool, we said... we didn't want to shop them to the police or to their rivals. We just wanted to talk, to hear what they had to say. They took us into the back room of a bar around the corner from the stadium. They were in disguise, wrapped up like casual versions of Lawrence of Arabia – hoodies, baseball caps and scarves over their faces.

Their top boy seemed to be a guy wearing a Burberry scarf, shades and a woolly hat. He sat behind a table with four deputies and explained how he got into hooliganism. 'Right in the beginning we modelled ourselves on the English,' he said. 'You see the hooligans on telly and you see Tottenham beat up Feyenoord in their own stadium and you love it... and you want to do that too.'

He told us he joined the F-Side almost by default – like all the lads the football came first, and after years of dedicated service on the terraces, the step up to becoming part of the firm seemed a natural one. 'I want to fight you, you want to fight me, what's the problem? Maybe you win, maybe I win, that's the risk I take. I love it.'

If the F-Side pride themselves on their refusal to work with any other firms, they have also established a name as ruthless opponents. In 1987 they sealed that reputation in an explosive fixture with Den Haag. Cruyff's side included

Marco van Basten, Marc Bosman and a young Dennis Bergkamp. By half-time Bosman had given the visitors a 2-0 lead – but the game would never be resumed.

As the players sucked oranges in the dressing room, Den Haag's Zuiderpark stadium erupted – the F-Side smashed through their barriers and met Den Haag's Northside hooligans head-on. The air was black with rocks, sticks, flags, seats... the ground was slick with mud and blood. The two firms crashed into each other with everything they had – knuckles and cheekbones split as fists connected, blood was spilled as knives were pulled out, limbs cracked as rioters crumpled under the weight of flung seats and volleyed lumps of wood.

Oh, and the Ajax crew lobbed a couple of homemade bombs into the mix too: their explosions added to the surreal horror of the TV images. On the news that night Holland watched dumbfounded at footage of ambulance men carrying motionless bodies through the smoke. It looked like something out of *Apocalypse Now*.

'Yeah it was great,' said our man in the Burberry scarf. 'They call it "The black day for football in Holland". It was great: we fucking kicked their arses, in their own stadium. It was on TV and in the papers and everything, my mum recognized me.'

A few years later they caught out Den Haag again. An enterprising Dutch TV company had the idea of a live studio debate between the top boys of all the main firms – a kind of tooled-up version of *Trisha*. Needless to say, a scornful F-Side declined the invitation... and then came anyway.

'There was a debate and Den Haag was there and Utrecht and the cockroaches of Feyenoord,' he remembered. After waiting until the programme was on-air, the F-Side stormed the studio. 'We went in through the windows and we fucking kicked their arses and the screen went all black,' he laughed. 'And the nicest thing is one of the cockroaches said: "I was looking death in the eyes", he had blood on his face and everything, fucking pussy.'

More recently, in 2005 Ajax hooligans wrecked two trains between Amsterdam and Rotterdam – and after disembarking, attempted to storm the Feyenoord stadium. The decision was taken to lock them out; the police waded in and in the resulting riot 47 officers were hospitalized and 43 members of the Ajax mob arrested.

Our boys shrug at the stories. The way they see it, the numbers are relatively small – and are nothing compared to the hatred they have for their Rotterdam rivals. Danny was interested in that hate; he asked them exactly what an Ajax v Feyenoord fixture meant to them.

'Do you have a Feyenoord fan here?' asked one of the lads, all in black with a checked scarf over his face.

'We can show you what it means,' said his friend, cracking his knuckles.

A fourth man spoke up – he wore a grey hoodie and, bizarrely, a Newcastle scarf. 'When Feyenoord is playing us, everybody goes,' he said. 'Even the old people who never go to football anymore, everybody is there. It is in your heart. You hate them so much you don't leave them alone, it is not possible. You have to be there.'

The main man explained. 'I can't sleep the night before. It's like, you already have adrenaline in your body then, you're looking forward to it so much. It's the biggest game we have, you know? And then on the day we'll meet early, we drink a lot and lots of guys take some drugs to be more aggressive and shit. I know it sounds crazy and maybe we are a bit crazy... but it's like fighting for your family, for your friends. It's the adrenaline thing with the bombs and the smoke and fighting for your life.'

The bomb thing kept coming up. Danny wanted to know – that's like, fireworks, right? Not actual bombs. A mistranslation.

Our man in Burberry shook his head. 'No it is not fireworks,' he said. 'I can show you a bomb if you want?'

And there it was – a stick of dynamite, just like you see in the movies. A slim tube about a foot long with a fuse sticking out of the end. He held it as casually as if it was a cigarette. 'When you see the smoke and you hear it: BANG! BANG! BANG! Fucking... it's great man,' he laughed, as our eyes popped wide.

'The people hear the bombs and everybody screams,' said the man in the Newcastle scarf, 'they love it. It gives a big bang and makes a little hole in the ground.'

'And if it hits someone it puts a hole in them?' asked Danny.

Everyone laughed. 'Probably.'

'And this adds to the atmosphere for you, yeah?' asked Danny, none of us quite believing that they were waving a stick of dynamite around. 'Having a, er, a bomb makes the whole ruck a little bit more lively?'

Burberry Scarf shrugged. 'Sure. When you hear the "boom!" it makes it all a bit more heavy, a bit bigger you know? Smoke and bombs and everything, tear gas and police. Sometimes it is real chaos and, yeah, it sounds stupid for people who don't know it, but it is a feeling, you know? It's a feeling.

'Listen,' he said, as the dynamite was pocketed again. 'For us, this is a war. It is a fucking war. When you are in a battle and you hear the bombs around you and you see the smoke... it is like you have to fight for your life and you look around and it's totally war, totally chaos. It never gets out of you. It never stops.'

• • •

We left the F-Side in the shadow of the Amsterdam Arena and headed back to the tourists and coffee shops. We might have had more frightening encounters than being with the Ajax firm – we never actually felt like we were in danger of anything other than being blown up accidentally – but the intensity of their hatred for Feyenoord was the equal of anything else we'd seen.

And nobody was expecting a bomb to be produced.

We were bound for Rotterdam the very next day for the Feyenoord/Ajax game... but we hadn't told the F-Side boys that. Mostly because we weren't going with them: our tickets were in the home end. We couldn't help wondering if we'd be seeing that same stick of TNT again – and how many other bombs might be lobbed in our direction.

Before we left we had the rest of the afternoon in Amsterdam and Peter wanted to record some more links. After the shambolic nature of the last lot, he had a new idea.

'Bicycles!' he said.

We all got bikes in the end: Stan's had a big bucket on the front like a bulldozer into which we piled all the camera gear; Danny chose a nice shiny red number with white handlebars. We found a spot by one of the canals on the edge of the Red Light District and watched as Danny cycled back and forth in the lane on the edge of the water. Peter had told him to ad lib, freestyle, say whatever came into his head: he followed him with the camera, leaning on Stan's bucket bike for support.

Danny kept cracking up. 'I'm here on my bike,' he started, 'trying to find out how they have a tear up in this town.' He gestured at the canal and wobbled over the road. 'It's so small and there's plenty of rivers to chuck people in and bridges to chuck them off...'

Peter wanted more local colour. 'And they're canals Danny, not bloody rivers,' he called, flicking the camera on as Danny pedalled towards us again.

'Local colour, you say? Check out the old brass over there with her bangers out,' he grinned. 'You can't film it but take my word for it they're a nice big pair of bangers.' He tried to put his hands in his mouth to whistle and veered straight into the path of a moped attempting to overtake him. It was being ridden by a pensioner; as he passed he shouted something. 'I used to have a bit of edge about me, you know,' said Danny, 'I was quite a cool actor... I am now on a red bike and nearly got run over by an 80-year-old man...'

Peter laughed and looked at Stan. 'What do you reckon we get some shots of the girls in the windows there?' Filming the prostitutes was strictly forbidden – we had been warned that if a pimp caught us at it things could get nasty. But then apart from the disappearing moped the only other people around were a couple of bums hunched over in an alley opposite.

'Fuck it,' said Stan, 'go for it, I say.'

Danny cycled past for another take as Peter kept the camera trained on the windows. Inside them, silhouetted against a pink/red backdrop, half-naked girls sat and listlessly smoked cigarettes, or fiddled with bra straps. Business was slow.

'Alright geezer!' shouted Danny as he passed the tramps. One of them looked up. The other looked over at us, Peter still leaning against Stan's bike with his camera fixed on the girls. The tramps started shouting. Suddenly from behind them a man appeared holding what could only be a crack pipe. He started shouting in Dutch, then bent down, picked up something from the floor and threw it at Danny. He ducked and it whistled over his head.

'Fuck me!' yelled Danny and pedalled right past as the man started running towards us. 'I'm only being attacked by a crack-selling pimp!'

Nobody moved for a second... and then we panicked. Peter jumped into the big bucket on the front of Stan's bicycle, cradling his camera like a baby. 'Go!' he shouted, and we all took off down the road, Stan sweating and heaving and swearing as he struggled to pick up speed. Behind us our pursuer kept shouting, kept hurling stones. As we eased away, Stan risked a look back before collapsing over his handlebars.

We caught up with Danny a few blocks down the road. He was in stitches. 'Who said the Dutch were laid back?' he laughed. 'In the space of a couple of hours I've been shown a bomb and been chased by a pimp on crack...'

• • •

If Amsterdam was all fun and games, things got serious in Rotterdam. The differences between the two cities go beyond football rivalry, they're deeply ingrained in the nation's psyche. They're only 50 miles apart, but it can feel like two different countries. If Amsterdam is the city of culture and tourists, of wealth and leisure, Rotterdam is the workhorse. Industrial and unglamorous, its residents nurse a resentment of their more cosmopolitan neighbours. Especially as the rise of Holland's capital as a centre for culture and tourism has mirrored a decline in the traditional industries – and a resulting decline in the fortunes of Rotterdam. Life is hard in Holland's second city. There are no tourists here – there's not much for them to see anyway.

We arrived ahead of the Ajax mob, in a little hire car with Peter at the wheel, still buzzing from the chase of the previous afternoon. The good mood wasn't to last too long. Our tickets for the match had come through official Feyenoord channels and despite the best efforts of our boys on the ground here, the local firms weren't going to play ball. They weren't being funny about it, they just weren't interested. We were going to see the most volatile derby in Dutch football – but we were going to have to make do with seats in the family stand. Gutted.

Still – there was always the atmosphere outside the ground to soak up. And there at least, the Rotterdam crowds didn't disappoint. They stood in packs of anything from a dozen to a hundred strong, filling the concrete spaces around the stadium with angry knots of colour, taunting the police, waiting for a glimpse of Ajax, itching for a chance to have a go at their most hated opponents.

If the F-Side had given us a taste of the rivalry that exists between the two cities, Feyenoord themselves have a serious pedigree for violence. They were the first Dutch supporters to be on the receiving end of football hooliganism, when Spurs took the city in 1974 – and it seems that night gave them a taste for trouble.

Nine years later they got payback: when Spurs returned for another European tie, Feyenoord had firmed up. They took the North Londoners by surprise – three of them were stabbed as the Dutch both took their revenge for 1974 and showed they'd learned a thing or two since then as well.

Feyenoord were there when Dutch hooliganism really came to the attention of the world. In October 1989, just one month after Ajax were banned from Europe after an iron bar was thrown at the Austria Vienna goalkeeper during a UEFA cup match, the Dutch champions hosted Feyenoord. The stadium was packed beyond capacity: kick off was delayed by 15 minutes as fans squeezed through the turnstiles, the terraces heaved and swelled with the prospect of trouble. Everyone knew it was going to go off – the only question was how, and how badly.

Midway through the first half Ajax scored – and it was like lighting the blue touch paper. Almost immediately there was an explosion from one of the stands, followed by screams. The first of two nail bombs had been thrown from the visitors' section – the second followed soon after. As the Ajax crowds went ballistic, riot police stormed the Feyenoord end – and were met head-on by hooligans carrying what weapons they could get their hands on. First aid teams struggled to make their way through the smoke, truncheons and missiles to where the bombs had exploded; all around them three-way running battles between Ajax, riot police and Feyenoord continued long after the final whistle and through all Amsterdam that night.

Fourteen fans had been injured by the Feyenoord nail bombs – tight packets of high explosive and lumps of metal. The local news that night described them as having the effect of hand grenades. One fan remained in a critical condition for days after an artery was severed by a piece of shrapnel.

Even the BBC got the message: 'Holland is fast taking over

as Europe's most troubled footballing nation,' the corporation gravely announced. But the Dutch firms had barely started.

Through the early 90s the travelling Feyenoord firms enjoyed massive clashes in European matches as well as domestically – taking out Stuttgart, Leverkusen, and most notably Monchengladbach, where 15,000 fans rioted across the city, completely overpowering stunned local police.

In 1997 the rivalry between Feyenoord and Ajax came to its inevitable climax: with murder.

On 23 March, Ajax and Feyenoord fans clashed in what became known as 'The Battle of Beverwijk'. The two teams weren't even playing each other – but their firms had come together nonetheless, in a field near the town of Beverwijk, just outside Amsterdam.

The Ajax F-Side were led by their top boy, Carlo Picornie – but they were surprised by a better-armed Feyenoord firm. As the two mobs tore into each other, the fight quickly escalated way beyond fists and boots. Knives, hammers, chains, baseball bats, Molotov cocktails, even electric stun guns were all seized by police afterwards – and when the dust had settled, Carlo Picornie was found dead. Feyenoord hooligans had smashed his head in with a hammer and as he fell to the floor stabbed and beat him with Stanley knives and a bicycle chain.

Two years later another riot in Rotterdam ended with the police opening fire, gunning down and injuring four Feyenoord fans. It took the rest of the night before order was finally restored.

And there's no sign of them easing off anytime soon. As we were there Feyenoord were serving out a UEFA ban: their visit to AS Nancy in France in November 2006 resulted in thousands of the firm smashing a glass partition between themselves and the French fans and storming into the home crowd. The match was suspended for half an hour as police with tear gas and full riot gear tried to regain control of the ground; the trouble continued afterwards as the Dutch hooligans laid waste to the French town.

If we were gutted that we wouldn't be meeting their top boys, we at least wanted to drink in some of the supercharged atmosphere around the stadium before the match.

The Old Bill weren't taking any chances. If the sharp rise in hooliganism here caught them napping at first, they're making up for it now. And for a match like this they were giving it everything they had. Helicopters buzzed overhead, mounted police patrolled the lines between the stadium and the train station that would bring the Ajax fans in. Slavering Alsations strained at their leashes and riot vans were parked every couple of hundred yards along the road. Behind the horses and dogs and vans were long, thick, black lines of riot police, sticks and shields at the ready, deathly quiet.

By contrast, the Feyenoord boys were in full voice. 'Rot-ter-dam!' they sang. 'Hoo-li-gan! Rot-ter-dam! Hoo-li-gan!'

Suddenly a roar went up. The Ajax trains had arrived and there was a push towards the station. The police were ready and the push was met by a bigger push back. Faced with the horses and dogs there was no way through and the mob broke up again, having to content themselves with hurling verbals across to the visitors – who, hemmed in by more police themselves, were doing the same. It was as close as the two firms got to each other.

Were we disappointed? On the one hand we hadn't come here for polite chit-chat and good behaviour but on the other hand the thought of nail bombs was still pretty clear in our minds. 'Shrapnel,' said Peter. 'You don't go to a match expecting to come away with shrapnel, do you?'

On the pitch the Rotterdam side took a pasting – 4-0 in the end. It was frustrating for the home fans and, barring one brief scuffle where they managed to break through the barriers and have a go at the Ajax fans, it was also pretty frustrating for their firm. So efficient was the policing that for the most part the whole thing went off like a children's party – albeit a children's party with some bad language and a lot of riot police.

'Let's get a drink,' said Danny, as we left the stadium.

● ● ●

Things got worse.

We drove to Den Haag the next day and after dropping our gear at the hotel did what all good Englishmen do when they're abroad: we headed for the nearest bar. We had high hopes for this town. Rotterdam felt like a bit of a washout: sure, the atmosphere around the ground was intimidating and the local boys made all the right noises... but there wasn't exactly much in the way of action. And nobody from their firm was willing to actually sit down and talk to us.

The Northside of Den Haag, on the other hand, had a reputation as being a little bit more out of control than the other Dutch firms, a little bit wilder. Coming from a club not swollen with the success of Ajax or Feyenoord meant that they had to try a little bit harder to make a name for themselves. And they've certainly done that – refusing even to take second best from the team itself. Following their relegation in 1982, the firm set fire to the monumental main stand of Zuiderpark Stadium, burning down an edifice that had stood since 1925.

It's an old fashioned, working class football club – some have even called Den Haag the Millwall of Holland. Danny was looking forward to meeting them.

When Peter joined us in the bar, he had a face like thunder. 'Fucking hell,' he swore as Stan put a beer in front of him. He downed it and swore again. Stan got another. He downed that too. 'We've got a problem,' he eventually said.

Peter had got back to his hotel room to find a message from the Northside. It seemed they weren't happy: they'd got wind of our chat with the Ajax firm and suddenly they didn't want to play any more. Not only that – it turned out that by even meeting the F-Side at all, we'd somehow allied ourselves with Den Haag's most hated enemy.

'It's like this,' he said. 'We can stay here in Den Haag... but the Northside, and I quote, "can't guarantee our safety". Whatever that means.'

'It means they're going to jump us,' muttered Stan.

'Does it? Or does it mean they're just fronting up a bit, giving it some of that to make a point?' Peter shrugged. 'Who knows? But can we take the chance?'

We couldn't understand their thinking. We thought we knew the score – and that the firms we had been in contact with knew the score too. In every country we visited the brief was always the same: meet one firm, then the other. We didn't take sides, we didn't judge, we treated everyone with respect – and we gave everyone the same platform. Of course we talked to the F-Side. We couldn't come to Holland and not at least try to hook up with Ajax's top firm.

But then there's recent bad blood between these two outfits. It's not like the ancient hatred of Chelsea/Spurs, say, or Liverpool/Man United. These wounds are fresh. They still hurt.

The rivalry might have started in 1987 when the bombs of the F-Side took apart Den Haag's Zuiderpark, but recent events have seen a vicious escalation in hostilities.

In January 2005 the Ajax Supporters' Home, their officially-sanctioned clubhouse and unofficial headquarters, went up in flames. There was no doubt it was arson – and for the F-Side, there was no doubt it was Den Haag who were responsible. Nobody has ever been officially charged for the blaze, so the F-Side took things into their own hands.

Thirteen months later, in February 2006, a mobbed-up Ajax stormed the Den Haag Supporters' Home – 70 F-Siders wielding knives and baseball bats rushed the building, stabbing two fans and destroying everything inside, before setting the clubhouse alight. The resulting inferno razed it to the ground, and according to some of the Northside, the F-Side hooligans even tried to set fire to injured fans as they lay bleeding.

The city went crazy. Thousands of furious Den Haag fans took to the streets demanding justice; police blocked all the motorways between the two cities. The government declared a state of emergency and Ajax fans were banned from the following game at Den Haag. Ten men were subsequently arrested... but for the Northside it's nowhere near enough. They have sworn revenge.

'It's basically a no no, isn't it?' said Danny. 'That's the level of hate between these clubs: just because we've even spoke to Ajax, they won't have anything to do with us.'

'And we're potentially a target ourselves now,' added Stan.

We checked out of the hotel and piled back in the car. What else could we do?

The Bunnikside of Utrecht – 'Don't think. Just do it.'

We didn't hang around Den Haag. What was the point of

staying in a town where we could be marked men? It might have been a lot of talk... but on the other hand, none of us fancied being found face down in a canal.

Holland, it had to be said, was turning into a bit of a pain in the arse. Ever since that pimp had chased us by the canal, yelling and waving his crack pipe as Stan cycled for his life, things had gone wrong.

We had one hand left to play. It was all down to Utrecht. And thankfully, Utrecht came good for us.

We had arranged to meet their firm, the Bunnikside, at the stadium itself. This was a mob with connections: Utrecht was the first club to build a Supporters' Home, they were the first club to try to work with the hooligans. The result? A firm with unparalleled access to the inner machinations of the club; and, in a geezer calling himself Bobby, a president of the Official Supporters' Club who also happens to be one of Holland's most respected hooligans. 'I represent 6,000 fans and about 300 hooligans,' he told us, matter-of-factly. When Danny laughed, trying to imagine a similar situation in the Premiership, Bobby looked confused. 'I think the main issue of having hooligans in the club is that we represent all the supporters. And it's possible for us to have our own security boys because we all know and have respect for each other.'

He shrugged. 'Follow me,' he said, 'I'll introduce you to some of our top boys, real bad men...'

The Utrecht mob may not have the numbers or the ordnance of Ajax or Feyenoord, but they're a naughty little outfit nonetheless.

In 1980 they even smashed up their own stadium. The old ground was due for demolition at the end of the season – the Bunnikside figured they'd save the club the trouble and do the job themselves. 'It's a job that was to take seven days and we did it in one hour,' they told us proudly. 'We destroyed the stadium with our bare hands.'

More recently, in 2002, they clashed with the capital city firm: after hijacking a couple of trains at Utrecht Central, demanding that they be provided with extra transport for the journey to Amsterdam – and, incredibly, getting them – they then ran rampant over the city itself. At the match, pockets of Bunnikside boys were scattered throughout the Amsterdam Arena, having bought tickets on the sly through official Ajax club cards. They quickly exploited their position, rampaging through the home terraces, laying into an initially-unaware F-Side. Once the local firm had got itself together and mounted a counter charge, the resulting fights grew so serious that the television coverage was interrupted as even the TV crews were forced to evacuate the stadium.

By the time the police had regained control, several of the Arena's toilets had been burnt out, most of the snack bars destroyed, seats and barriers ripped out and over 100,000 Euros of damage inflicted. One hundred fans had been arrested, countless more injured.

Inside their Supporters' Home – a massive bar, basically, with wooden beams in the ceiling from which hung scarves, shirts, banners and trophies from successful campaigns; as well as a dancefloor, a VIP area, and a total capacity of 1,500 – we were served pints of lager and taken to meet some Bunnikside veterans.

And a proper bunch of hardcore boys they looked too. The scars and wrinkles, the greying hair, the inky blue tattoos, even their clothes – faded denim and black jackets as opposed to the sharp Burberry and Lonsdale casual threads of the younger guys – all marked them out as an old-school mob. There were nine of them and they didn't bother with disguises, or false names. They sat on their terrace sucking on thin roll-ups and drinking lager. They watched as we approached, narrowed eyes taking us in for exactly what we were – too easy, too soft, to bother getting funny with.

At least, that's what we hoped.

'Alright lads,' said Danny, giving it the full swagger and front. 'Getting the beers in I see. Hope you can handle them, eh? I wouldn't want to have to sort you out or anything...'

Stan gulped. They laughed, and we breathed again.

'Especially not this one. Proper nutter,' he continued, pointing at one of the nastiest looking of them, a wiry, leathery man with heavy features, thick eyebrows and bad teeth. 'Proper mad boat on him! He could have a tear up and no two ways about it...'

The men kept laughing. All except the guy that Danny had probably just mortally offended. We quickly got on with it.

Pollie, a veteran Bunnikside top boy and a huge bulk of a man, grey hair tied back in a pony tail and scars on both cheeks, told us about the firm's pedigree. 'It all started in the early 70s,' he said, 'During the 70s we were the most feared football gang in the Netherlands, we were the first gang to use weapons. We liked to hit people with bicycle chains. We were famous for it; they called us the chain gang. But there are other weapons – bats, knives, Stanley knives, bottles, anything that can be used...

'If you want to do some damage to someone else, you have to do it fast, and you have to use something that's going to get you a result. So almost everyone now uses weapons.'

Almost all of the boys there had scars; Danny wanted to

know how serious their injuries had been. A guy calling himself Johnnie unzipped his jacket and showed us a ragged white line running across the length of his chest.

'It was half-time and they came on,' he said, 'all these Feyenoord supporters, they came into our territory... so we go downstairs to meet them and I have my bicycle chain. I'm in there a while, hitting some guys and I go back to the stand and they say: "hey John you are bleeding'. It's only then I realize they have stabbed me.'

Johnnie had also been imprisoned for hooliganism – he served time with the heavily set man Danny had earlier offended. 'We were there for three months,' he shrugged, 'for fighting against Ajax. There were also Ajax supporters in the same place... but they don't want to fight with us in the prison.'

Everyone laughed. 'I'm not bleeding surprised,' said Danny.

Pollie spoke up again: 'The firm has changed because of better police surveillance. In the old days you'd simply step off the train and have some fun. Then the police got wise, so you have to find other ways to meet your opponents, it's a sort of cat and mouse game. Nowadays it's popular to not fight your opponent on the day of the match but a day or two before, or at house parties, or at festivals. In fact, we don't really get to meet each other at football stadiums so much anymore.'

'That is the problem now,' said Johnnie, shaking his head. 'The day of the game there are so many police that we cannot start a proper fight.'

Another of the old firm, a man in an army jacket and a black woolly hat with bulging eyes and a habit of jabbing his finger as he spoke, told us of his own favourite football memory.

'In my younger days, when I was 18 or 19 years old,' he began, 'there was a train coming to Utrecht full of the

Feyenoord hooligans. And they were leaning out of the windows, shouting at us, calling us names. We were standing there by the rail track, with bottles filled with petrol and oil – that's the best mixture to keep it burning. So they come by and I saw them all, the fuckers... and then their shouting changed to screaming. Why? Because we'd thrown the bottles and the train was burning, that's why! And it was burning all the way into the station...'

Pollie and Johnnie and the rest all laughed, their faces wistful for the good old days when you could petrol bomb trains without undue pressure from the authorities.

Things are different now. The Bunnikside may have been the first firm to get their own Supporters' Home, but following further clashes with the F-Side and the Northside, the police have got them marked. Bobby pointed out 'hidden' cameras in the rafters of the bar and told us that some hooligans had even been arrested on evidence secured by police surveillance. Danny asked him if that was the case, why didn't the authorities simply shut them down?

He grinned. 'We are still open because they know that if we were closed, they would have 1,500 boys waiting outside... and they would have a lot more problems than now.'

Nonetheless, the cameras do have some effect on curtailing the activities of the old guard. 'It is very tricky to get involved in incidents now because they know you,' said Theo, another Bunnikside veteran. 'The police know all the guys now.' He winked. 'But now there is a new group coming, we call it the third or fourth generation, and they don't know these guys. They are different guys, younger guys...'

We left the veterans to their memories and their lagers and Bobby introduced us to the top boy of this new breed, this kind of Utrecht baby squad. He was a kid in his twenties with sharp features and a Lacoste cap; rather than having the solid bulk of the old boys, he looked like he knew his way around the gym. He called himself Rowdy and all the time he talked to us his eyes never left Danny's.

The way it worked, he told us, was that he was in constant contact with the rival firms – by mobile phone mostly, as email was too easy for the police to trace – and between them they would work out a venue to meet. Away from the Old Bill, away from the football even, they could concentrate on the basics: kicking the shit out of each other.

'I'm happy if we can get a straight fight anywhere,' he said, 'even if it's just 40 against 40. I hate them all. Ajax, Feyenoord, Den Haag... I hate them all. It's only Utrecht.'

And even if these confrontations are not quite the thousand-strong riots of old, they at least fall below the police radar and can be every bit as vicious.

'All of the youngsters are using weapons,' Rowdy told us. 'If you are in a large group and there's guys coming at you, what are you going to do? Fight with your hands? We have to use weapons.'

Danny asked if Rowdy was worried about going too far, if one day he would end up seriously injuring or even killing someone. He asked if he ever thinks about that.

Rowdy grinned: 'Don't think,' he said. 'Don't think. Just do it. It's normal for us. If you are worried then you shouldn't get involved. You know what you are up to.'

And that's the modern face of liberal Holland: bombs, arson and stabbings. Not thinking – just doing. It could only end in more murder. 'Sex, drugs and clogs my arse,' muttered Stan as he switched off the camera.

CHAPTER FIVE

BRAZIL

Brazil – the greatest footballing nation on earth. A country that moves to the rhythm of the beautiful game, that lives and breathes football. A country that bleeds football. Not only did Brazil reinvent the game but they reinvented the way fans supported their team. It was here that football fanaticism was born: while everyone else was politely applauding goals, Brazil brought colour, noise and passion to the game. It was here that the carnival first came to football.

But there is a dark side too.

The nation that brought us the greatest team the world has ever seen – the 1970 World Cup side – has also taken football violence to unparalleled heights. They set new standards here, on and off the pitch.

You've got to get in there, get past the keepy-uppy tricks for the tourists, the guided tours and the sanitized samba of upmarket Rio. You've got to get down in the favelas, among the wild shanty kids, down where football really is a matter of life or death and days are defined by sun, soccer, samba

and shootings. These are the most fanatical fans on earth –
men and boys with guns who aren't afraid to kill and to die
for their cause.

We were going into the most violent ghettoes on the planet
– and, in a speeding bus on the outskirts of Rio with a firm
from Palmeiras of Sao Paulo, we were going to see for
ourselves exactly how it feels to come under gunfire.

We all prepared for Brazil in different ways. Danny had some
DVDs of the glory teams of the 1970s and 80s – Pele,
Rivelino, Zico, Socrates, he became obsessed with Socrates,
for some reason; Peter had a book about the history of
Brazilian football. Stan had a DVD too: he watched *City of*
God four times straight, back to back, on the long flight from
Amsterdam to Rio de Janeiro. By the time we crossed the
equator he was so familiar with the story of gangs and drugs
and guns in the shanty towns that he could practically speak
the language himself.

We were beginning to worry a little bit about Stan.

We may have each had our own way of preparing for
Brazil, but there was no doubting that everyone was
especially excited about this one. It wasn't just that we were
football fans coming to the spiritual home of the beautiful
game; nor was it that – like everyone else we knew – we'd
been raised on images of green numbers on golden shirts, of
impossibly fluid runs and silky dribbles, of bending free
kicks and extravagant flicks and skills we would spend hours
trying to recreate in the playground; of course, it was all
these things – but it was something else too.

We all felt that Brazil was going to be a turning point in our
round-the-world adventure. It was the first time we'd left

THE REAL FOOTBALL FACTORIES

Europe, for a start, and if we were swapping the grey damp of a European winter for the clear skies and golden sun of summer in South America, we also knew that the weather was going to be the least of the differences in store for us. Everything was different down here – the football, the culture, even the way people thought. It was all so much more vivid, more colourful, more upfront and in your face. One of the production crew had told us before we left that once you've experienced Brazil, nothing ever seems the same again... and we couldn't wait to see so for ourselves.

As we landed, Danny announced he would not be shaving the whole time we were in Brazil. He was going to grow a beard. Like Socrates.

•••

Brazil is a massive country – the fifth largest in the world and near enough the size of mainland Europe. Its environment, population and culture are so diverse, you could spend decades here just trying to soak up the contrasts – and we could have spent years just uncovering the football culture alone.

We had about a week – no time for jetlag, let alone any kind of cultural understanding. We were here to visit three cities, catch up with five football firms, see a match, and maybe, if we were lucky, find time for a cocktail or two along the way.

Our plans were going to change, like always. What we didn't realize is just what that change would lead to.

For the moment, however, things started beautifully. Our hotel in Rio was bang on Copacabana beach and we barely paused to dump the gear, strip off the jeans and head for the deckchairs. As we all ordered caiparinhas – generous shots of cachaca, a Brazilian rum made of fermented cane juice, with zingy fresh limes and lots of sugar – laid back and watched the booty girls sashay past in the flimsiest bikini bottoms, Peter laid out the agenda. First thing, he said, was a trip to the Maracana. No hooligans, no nasty geezers with scarves on their faces and weapons in their pockets, no wild-eyed boys talking about their hatred and their passion, no constantly feeling like any minute they were going to turn that intensity on to us... no tension and no fear. We were going to the Maracana as fans. Our first day in Brazil was strictly *turista*.

After that Peter started talking about the rest of the week, but no one was really listening. A couple of girls who looked like Destiny's Child after major enhancement surgery were playing beach volleyball and every one of our eyes followed them.

'Wow,' breathed Stan, mouth open.

'Nice ball control,' nodded Danny, sipping at his cocktail. 'Very nice indeed.'

•••

We were taken around the Maracana with the other tourists, and if we took just as many pictures as all the others, if we felt just as excited and awestruck and enthusiastic about the history of the magnificent stadium, if we queued up with the others to put our feet into the imprints of Ronaldo's and the rest, we also felt a little detached from them. These tourists were family-stand types, nice people with good values, the kind who watch Sky on Sunday afternoons and take their kids to international games.... the kind who welcome all-seater stadiums and CCTV and stronger policing on matchdays. Which, in a way, you can't argue with. The only thing was we were seeing past all that now. Or at least, we weren't used to it anymore.

When we looked around this temple to Brazilian football – and even with its capacity halved from 200,000 for the 2014 World Cup bid it is still the greatest football stadium on earth, no contest – we got the goose bumps alright... but we also saw the terraces for what they were. Rio de Janeiro is one of the most violent places on earth – and right here is one of the natural flashpoints for trouble. When we gazed around the vast bowl of the Maracana we didn't just see a theatre of football – we saw a stage on which far more brutal and deadly dramas were played out. Week after week.

And increasingly, they involve guns.

Brazil is a society with its finger on the trigger. In 2005 in London there were 175 murders: in the same year in Rio there were 6,620. Nationally, the statistics go crazy: every year some 40,000 people die from firearms incidents in this country. That's over 100 every single day. In the last 25 years over half a million people have been killed due to gun crime and over 200,000 of them have been adolescents. And it's reckoned that 90 per cent of the guns in circulation – some 15 million at a conservative estimate – are in the hands of the general public. Which means more often than not, owned by the kind of lads who come to cheer on their teams at the Maracana.

For those living in the extreme poverty of the *favelas*, the ramshackle, tumbledown shanty towns thrown up sometimes literally next to plush apartment blocks and million dollar mansions, a gun is not only a status symbol, it's a means of getting what you want – or even of simply staying alive. Take that kind of desperation, throw the passion and pride of South American football into the mix and you've got serious action. There have been at least 70 murders officially attributed to football violence in Brazil since the mid-80s: talk to any firm and they'll tell you the figure is much higher.

The Maracana is a Mecca for football, certainly. But it's also a symbol for something else entirely.

Back in the stadium itself, Danny was warming up, talking to a guide about the dressing rooms. 'So old Socrates would have got his thighs rubbed down there then?' he winked. 'Nice massage, ease the tension?'

We all stopped opposite a wall depicting the greatest players to have graced the famous Maracana pitch. They were all here – Danny's Socrates of course, Pele, Garrincha, Romario, Beckenbauer...

'Beckenbauer?' shouted Stan. 'Franz Beckenbauer? What the fuck is Franz Beckenbauer doing here?' He looked furious.

Some of the other tourists backed away. Peter sighed. It was time to get back to work.

The Raca Rubro Negra of Flamengo – 'They're all armed.
It can get out of control and there's nothing the police
can do...'
Our brief time as tourists was over. Cocktails and guided tours were all well and good but we were itching to get behind the polished exterior and into the real business of football support in this town. And in Rio de Janeiro, that means Flamengo.

THE REAL FOOTBALL FACTORIES

Flamengo are Brazil's most supported team – with something like 33 million fans, that's roughly the equivalent of the entire adult population of the UK. But if their support is vast and nationwide, here in their hometown, their hardcore followers come straight from one of the city's most notorious neighbourhoods.

Vas Lobo is a district in the south of Rio with a reputation as one of the most dangerous *favelas* in South America. To grow up there is to grow up in some of the most extreme poverty in the world – and also to grow up amid casual bloodshed and deprivation on a scale that makes the streets of Deptford, Moss Side or Toxteth look like Millionaires' Row.

This was the real City of God. Ruled by the drug gangs, those streets are off-limits to all but those unlucky enough to have been born there. Even the police stay away – except on rare military-style 'invasions', massive semi-official operations where suspected gang members are rounded up and murdered. In one such incident, a police death squad killed 21 men and boys in the slum in retaliation for the deaths of four policemen by the drug gangs.

Drugs may rule the *favelas*, but football gives the people hope. What schools exist here provide only the most basic of education and nobody gets Jobseekers' Allowance. Only football provides anything like an escape route. Watching football, supporting football, playing football.

Every boy dreams of playing his way out of the shanty towns. But for all except one in a million – like Adriano, the Inter Milan striker, whose gift with the ball saw him dribble his way out of the slums all the way to the 2006 World Cup – there is no escape from the *favelas*. If you're born in Vas Lobo, you die in Vas Lobo: if you're lucky, not before you're 30.

Nobody chooses to come here. But, like the song says, fools rush in where angels fear to tread. And our trouble began before we even got near the place.

The road to Vas Lobo is known as the Gaza Strip – it acts as the border between two other *favelas*, Vigario Geral and neighbouring Parada de Lucas. The two have been at war for years, waging an ongoing conflict over drug territory that has claimed the lives of hundreds, and it is not unusual for innocent passers-by to be killed in the crossfire that is an almost daily occurrence across the road.

We were told by our team over here that there was no way we were going to drive ourselves, and then our driver – a massive geezer with missing teeth and a pistol under his seat – told us that it was probably best we turned the cameras off. And then hid them. And then hid ourselves. When cars weren't being shot at, he explained, they were often ambushed and hijacked by the gangs.

In 2002, he told us, a Brazilian reporter found secretly filming in the *favelas* was hacked to death with a samurai sword… and then burnt in a shallow grave. But we should be alright, he said, so long as no one saw us or our gear.

'Isn't the dangerous bit supposed to be actually meeting the firms?' asked Danny. 'Not the journey there?' He looked around. We were already crouched under our seats. 'And where do Brazilian slum kids get hold of a samurai sword, anyway?'

Stan motioned for him to get his head down. 'Japanese tourists,' he whispered, and made a cutting motion across his throat.

If the journey to the home of the Flamengo firm was intense enough, Peter reminded us that once we arrived we were going to be in the heart of the *favela*. 'Nothing but respect,' he said, 'we're guests here and we should be alright. But we show them nothing but respect. This is their manor and they're top of the food chain.'

We were met by the top boy of Flamengo's main firm. Paulo is the president of Raca Rubro Negra, or the Red and Black Race, named after Flamengo's distinctive club colours. As he led us through dusty streets where the houses stood lopsided and mostly, it seemed, home-built, past barefoot kids running at top speed and skinny, wild-eyed dogs chasing their own tails, he explained how for the lads in areas like this, belonging to the firm can be the only thing worth living for.

'Flamengo comes first,' he said, 'before anything else in life. The Flamengo supporters came from the slums and the hills, from the poorest areas. Our biggest passion is our firm. It is a feeling of honour, it is the same feeling we have towards our family, our parents. It is a strong feeling of love.'

That passion is expressed through membership of Raca Rubro Negra – and, as we approached their headquarters, we began to see, and to hear, just how.

It wasn't even matchday, yet the building that Paulo and his firm used as an unofficial bar and clubhouse was swathed in flags and banners. On the pavement outside a massive banner stretched 100 feet or so down the road... but the noise could be heard from miles away.

It sounded like an earthquake, or a tidal wave – a solid rumble – and as we got closer it became a deafening roar that we felt deep in our guts. Paulo grinned as we were handed plastic cups of beer; he slapped Danny on the back. 'Inside,' he shouted, 'inside!'

Inside the clubhouse was like being within the bass bin of a speaker at the loudest rave ever staged. The room – a concrete shell decorated with red and black flags and elaborate graffiti – was packed with men, most of them banging drums, everyone dancing. The walls shook from the noise.

We couldn't help ourselves – we joined in, arms above our heads, grins on our faces. This was what we'd come to see, this was Brazil: a million times more authentic than caiparinhas on Copacabana beach or guided tours of the Maracana. Here we were, in the heart of the shanty towns, dancing to samba with a firm from Flamengo. It felt like we'd finally arrived.

'Unbelievable,' shouted Danny at Paulo. 'Mindblowing! It's non-stop, there's not a break in it. What can I say? What a welcome that is, what a welcome, I feel like I've had about eight Es! You lot wouldn't even have to hit your rivals – you could drum them to death!'

In a quieter back room – we could hear each other if we yelled in one other's ears – Paulo explained: 'The *carioca* [people from Rio] are very festive and are passionate about football – and in football we have samba, carnival. And the Raca Rubro Negra are very festive!' He waved a finger. 'We go along to support our team but fights do break out. Fights happen outside and spread.'

Increasingly, these fights are proving fatal. When Flamengo recently defeated local rivals Vasco da Gama in the Maracana stadium, 18-year-old Rodrigo Cunha Coutinho was rushed to the hospital after being nearly beaten to death. Worse was to come. Fellow Flamengo fan Flavio Augusto Marinho, 14, was shot and killed as the rival firms clashed at different points around the city after the game.

'Generally, we have to fight to defend ourselves any which way we can,' explained Paulo. 'Here in Rio, in the past there have been fights but they were fought with their fists, without cowardice... not with firearms. Today it's complicated, they're all armed. It can get out of control and there's nothing the police can do.'

He topped up our beer and gestured back into the main room where his boys were still kicking up a storm on the drums. 'We are very much a family,' he said, 'we're very much a tranquil firm. It's very chilled and everyone can participate. We all watch out for each other, we have that kind of ideology where we help out those who need it.'

But Paulo can't have a peaceful life because he's also head of the Raca Rubro Negra, and that means he can't avoid trouble. 'We have serious problems with Palmeiras' firm,' he said. 'Today our severe rivalry with Palmeiras stems from their cowardice in the 90s, when they ambushed some of our boys. Even though it was in the past, no one forgets. There's a lot of hate and bitterness.'

As we danced our way back out to the waiting car and got ready to duck under the seats for the return journey, we didn't tell Paulo that the boys from Palmeiras were to be our next stop.

The Mancha Verde of Palmeiras – 'All of us here are ready for anything: to fight, to kill, even to die'
Sao Paulo is the largest city in South America, with a population of 30 million. And like Rio, it is a city of fantastic wealth – alongside indescribable poverty. If it's lacking some

of the glamour of its northern neighbour, it more than makes up for it where football is concerned.

There are three major teams here – Corinthians, Palmeiras and Sao Paulo, but it was the first two that we were here for. Among Brazil's – and therefore the world's – elite teams, they've each won the Serie A championship four times. They also attract some of the country's most fanatical support.

Our boys here had fixed it for us to meet both outfits – in contrast to some of the other countries we'd been to, it seemed the hooligans out here were only too happy to talk – and first up was Palmeiras. Their firm, the Mancha Verde or Green Stain, is one of Brazil's naughtiest crews.

It turned out there were some conditions attached to our meeting, however. We were used to firms getting a little bit funny with us – changing the location of our interviews, disguising themselves, even ducking out of arranged meets altogether – but the Mancha Verde pulled a new one. They insisted we adhere to their dress code.

'Everyone has to wear green,' said Peter. 'I'm serious. And no black at all – not even socks.'

Stan started laughing. We'd been living out of suitcases for weeks now, recycling all our gear when we couldn't get to a washing machine. It was a good day that found us in clean clothes, never mind colour-specific outfits.

'I'm struggling for a pair of pants at the moment,' muttered Danny.

'Do you think they'll mind if my top's a bit creased?' asked Stan. 'Or is there a specific way we should iron those too?'

Nevertheless, we suited up – green t-shirts all round, shorts and Reeboks – and Stan's cockiness quickly disappeared once we'd been introduced to Janio, top boy and current president of the Green Stain. Wiry and intense, he's built like Amir Khan and is an expert in the martial art Muay Tai, a kind of ultra-aggressive form of kickboxing. 'Of course the physical side of this gives you an advantage over most people,' he said, eyeing up where Stan's beer gut spilled over his shorts. 'It's good to be taught discipline and respect for your betters – and to pass this on to the firm.'

Stan nodded, unconsciously smoothing out his creases as we followed Janio to his HQ.

Inside, the atmosphere grew. Everywhere was green – the walls, the blinds on the windows, even the light bulbs. The resulting tinge gave everything a kind of seasick feel; it made us a bit unsteady, a bit off-balance. Janio sat us down at a table at one end of the bar. He sat opposite us... and filed behind him in were rows of silent footsoldiers of the Green Stain. They filled the bar – there must have been 50 of them – lined up in their green shirts and green baseball caps; every single one of them was staring at us.

We were all sweating: Janio had a little smile on his face, the very picture of a reasonable man while the boys behind him looked about ready to riot. Danny cleared his throat. 'So how many of you boys are ready to fight for your club?' he asked. He made it sound like an invitation.

Every single hand in the room went up. 'All of us here are ready for anything: to fight, to kill, even to die,' said Janio. 'Our ideology is above everything else... We're prepared to abandon our families, leave our jobs, abandon everything to follow our club and defend our flag. Our firm was born to change Palmeiras' history. We were formed to fight. I find it difficult to believe that there is another firm like ours in the world. Everyone here is dangerous if you mess with us.'

'Fair enough, fair enough,' said Danny, with a nod. 'okay. Good answer.'

An illustration of just how dangerous the Mancha Verde can be was made clear to the entire country in 1994. At a junior match against Sao Paulo, the Palmeiras firm invaded the stadium, charging the police and the rival fans with iron bars, lumps of wood, rocks and bricks. In the resulting riot – raging the length of the stadium and across the whole pitch – 100 fans and 22 policemen were seriously injured and one fan was killed, beaten to death.

'Mancha Verde isn't violent,' insisted Janio. 'It's just violent when provoked. And in the past we also had to take action so people started respecting our identity. We have to arrive and leave wearing our shirts with our flag held high. It doesn't matter how many supporters turn up to fight us, we have to defend our shirt. If there's two of us, one of us will leave with the banner and the other will fight the masses. It doesn't matter if we are outnumbered.'

Danny wanted to know about guns. Janio shrugged. 'We are against firearms,' he said, 'but we know when we go to certain stadiums, like in Rio for example, they are cowards and they don't fight with their fists.

'Our ideology is that we are an organized firm, we are not gangsters. For us fighting is our way of defending our flag. It's what we like and what we want. Wood and rocks are a part of it. Guns on the other hand are a lot more dangerous. It's too easy to stand 100-200 metres away from your enemy and shoot them down.' He leaned forward and cracked his knuckles. 'But to physically fight the enemy,' he grinned, 'now that's what we like.'

The boys behind him murmured their approval.

But nonetheless, Brazilian hooligans are using guns – and the Green Stain know at first hand just how much they change the game.

Janio's predecessor as president of the Mancha Verde, Cleo, was killed by members of Gavioes da Fiel (or Hawks Of The Faithful), the top firm for local rivals Corinthians. He was ambushed and shot twice as he left the headquarters one night. And in 2005 Diobo Borges, a 23-year-old member of the Green Stain, died of massive haemoraging after being shot in the back as he got on a train – also the victim of Corinthians fans.

'They are the guys who showed us the value of the firm,' said Janio, 'they showed us that we must be prepared to die for it. They are our martyrs.'

We looked at the boys filling the room: they might have been mostly kids in their teens, but their eyes said it all. It was obvious to anyone that they were burning with a hunger, a fierce desire to prove themselves, to fight for their flag. We looked at them and we knew that Cleo and Diobo would not be the last of the firm to die in the line of duty.

As it turned out, we would come awfully close to being there when that next martyr was created. Before we left, Janio invited us to accompany the firm on their last away day of the season: they'd hired a coach and were mobbing up for the trip to Fluminese of Rio. We shook hands and told him we were in.

It was almost the worst decision of our lives.

We'd gone into the Mancha Verde manor unnerved by their intensity and commitment, and if we'd seen nothing but total belief from the boys in there – and in Janio just about the most focused leader of a firm that we'd encountered yet

– we also came out of their HQ almost looking forward to seeing them again.

'They were alright geezers,' nodded Danny, 'hearts in the right place, know what I mean?'

'How many of them will make it to our age?' wondered Stan, and then as Danny gave him a look, he shrugged. 'Seriously though, it's a different business here, isn't it? Different rules. Rucking in England is one thing – but you know you're not going to get shot, for fuck's sake. Some of those boys in there are going to get shot. Fact. And it's a bit fucking off, isn't it? What sort of person shoots people in the back...'

Peter interrupted him. 'Best not get too worked up about it,' he said. 'We're going to a party with their rivals tonight.'

The Gavioes da Fiel of Corinthians – 'I would kill, for sure. You have to kill...'
To say that Corinthians and Palmeiras are rivals is a bit like saying Rangers and Celtic tend to disagree a bit. They're not rivals: they are sworn enemies. They hate each other with an all-consuming passion. And matches between them are played to the highest stakes.

In 1974 the legendary midfielder Rivelino – national icon and member of the 1970 World Cup winning team – was kicked out of the club after one such fixture. 'I played for Corinthians against Palmeiras and we lost,' he remembered later, 'Everyone knew I had supported Palmeiras as a boy and so I got the blame. I was sacked.'

By today's standards, Rivelino can count himself lucky. More recently, defender Marquinhos received death threats after he conceded a penalty in a vital match against their local rivals – he was forced to leave the club for the safety of his wife and children.

Corinthians' top firm Gavioes da Fiel – or Hawks of the Faithful – have not claimed direct responsibility for the threats against Marquinhos... but they do have form for that kind of thing. In the late 1990s dissatisfied members of the firm even ambushed the Corinthians team coach as it returned from an away game, battering it with crowbars as the terrified driver sped off.

Safe to say they don't tolerate anything less than total commitment, then.

However, they do have a more community-minded side too. This was the team Socrates played most of his career for, after all, and, as far as Danny was concerned, that counted for a lot. And like the boys we had met in Flamengo, the Hawks were big on samba: in preparation for the annual Carnival, they came together every Friday to practice. Inevitably, these 'practices' lasted all night, involved the whole neighbourhood and turned into mini-carnivals in themselves. As it was Friday, we had been asked to come along.

We rolled up at 1am – there was no point in arriving any earlier, we were told, nothing really gets going until at least midnight – driven by yet another gun-packing friendly giant into *favela* streets that grew ever more empty of cars and ever more packed with people. They were all heading in the same direction, shuffling and swinging and dancing towards the noise, the irresistible drums. We followed them into a huge hangar.

Inside it was like Glastonbury crossed with the Shed End – with entertainment by the Moulin Rouge. The cavernous building heaved and shook with thousands of people beating drums, blowing whistles, shaking tambourines, dancing, drinking, snogging; drop-dead gorgeous girls wearing feathers in their hair and sparkling bikini bottoms shook their bootys in formation; a massive kind of haphazard conga ebbed and flowed around the place. Every single person was moving; every single person was making noise.

It was fucking brilliant. So brilliant, in fact, that it was easy to forget that we were in the presence of some of the nastiest hooligans on the planet.

This firm do things on a massive scale. In 1977 when they won the Serie A title, riots between jubilant Corinthians Hawks and furious Palmeiras fans escalated far beyond the powers of the police to deal with them – as many as 120,000 hooligans ran rampant through the city, whole neighbourhoods were destroyed. A year before, some 70,000 Corinthians fans made the six-hour trip up the motorway to the Maracana to see their team beat Fluminese in the league semi-finals: it was christened 'the invasion of Rio'.

More recently, the Hawks have flexed their muscles closer to home. In June 2006, they took on the Sao Paulo police force: thousands of them rushed the barriers at a home game, surprising the authorities. Before the police could get themselves together the Hawks had torn down the fencing and were on the pitch, laying into anyone in a uniform and using everything from rocks to whole advertising hoardings as weapons. Hundreds were hospitalized – and the police were completely overwhelmed. Some of the injured that night had gunshot wounds.

That same year, when Chelsea boss Jose Mourinho turned up to take a look at Carlos Tevez – then the Corinthians' star forward – he was forced to take cover in a dressing room, barricaded in for two hours after angry Hawks stormed the directors' box in an attempt to 'dissuade' the club from selling their best player.

'It was like being in the middle of a war zone – police were throwing gas bombs, the supporters were running all over the place and everything was in total chaos,' said River Plate president Jose Marie Aguilar. Mourinho and the Corinthians directors were eventually rescued by armed police; they had to escort the Chelsea boss all the way back to the airport.

Oh, and another thing. This firm claims to have 65,000 members. That's about two-thirds the official size of the British Army.

We were led through the crowd to the top boy of the Gavioes da Fiel. A short man with dark hair in a neat parting, he looked more like a regular city boy than most of the guys we'd met. He offered us all beers and shook everyone's hands and introduced himself as Pulguinha – meaning 'little flea'. Perhaps to make up for his lack of menace, he was sat next to a huge unshaven man with hooded eyes and enormous hands that looked like they could snap a spinal cord without breaking sweat. He looked us up and down slowly and then turned away. We were clearly considered no threat whatsoever.

'We are known as the biggest firm in Latin America,' said Pulguinha with a smile, like he was a salesman describing a successful business proposition. 'Because of our position, we have a certain responsibility. We have to apply rules to the violence. For example, we don't act, we react towards violence. We don't start the fights.'

We'd heard this before. Yeah... but the Hawks do get stuck in, ventured Danny. There have been incidents, shootings...

He shrugged. 'There's violence everywhere; accidents happen, deaths happen. This is Brazil, it happens.'

He smiled at Peter and stood up again. 'Is that good for you?'

Stan raised his eyebrows. Danny scratched his chin.

'Great, great,' said Peter. 'Do you mind if we walk around a little?'

We left Pulguinha and his patter and went after some of the rank-and-file Hawks footsoldiers. Even if the president of this firm did believe his own talk about applying rules to the violence, we reckoned that in a mob of 65,000 it was going to be pretty much impossible to get everyone singing from the same hymn sheet.

Sure enough, it didn't take long to uncover a few genuine headcases. Like the Green Stain boys, some of these had a certain glint in their eyes.

A man in a white t-shirt and a baseball cap gave Danny another can of lager and explained what being a member of the Gavioes meant to him: 'We are who we are,' he said, swaying slightly. Danny asked if he applied responsibility to his use of violence. He laughed. 'Our enemies need to watch out,' he said, 'because if they mess with us we will break their necks, we'll slice their necks off and we'll trample all over them. We've had hundreds of fights. We feed off our battles.'

Another man – he was a boy really, couldn't have been more than 17, dressed all in black, tall and lanky and still with acne scars on his cheeks – explained how fights were organized.

'We post the details on the internet and make calls,' he said. 'We arrange the fights for after the match, we set a time and a place and everyone turns up.'

And weapons?

'We take sticks, stones and bombs with us. We carry the bombs in our shirts, we pick up the wood and stones on the way there.'

Stan wanted to know if he was scared of dying. The tit for tat shootings between the big firms surely meant that it was only a matter of time before someone turned up to one of their organized fights packing serious firepower.

He stared at Stan, unblinking. 'Sometimes you're scared of dying,' he said, 'but during the fights you have to push that to the back of your mind. I have thought about the fact that I could kill someone else... but at the same time I could die too.

'If I had to kill, I would. Of course, I would, without a doubt. I would kill, for sure. You have to kill not to die.'

Danny asked him how that would make him feel.

He looked at us with no emotion in his eyes whatsoever. 'If it were the enemy I wouldn't feel a thing,' he said, and sauntered back towards the dancing throng.

● ● ●

Rio and Sao Paulo had been eye-openers for us. We knew that Brazil was a violent country, that the *favelas* were effectively ruled by the drugs gangs and that football was for most people the only escape from days dominated by poverty and danger – but what we didn't realize was just how much the casual gun culture of the shanty towns had infected the football terraces.

'Sun, samba and shootings,' was how someone had jokingly described Brazilian football support – we'd laughed at the time, but it didn't seem so funny any more.

Our next stop was 700 miles south, and the affluent city of Porto Alegre. There is a campaign here to gain independence from Brazil – and if in some ways the city did feel like it was in a different country; there were some inescapable similarities.

Porto Alegre is a city divided – not so much alongside rich/poor lines as in Sao Paulo or Rio de Janeiro – but in strictly footballing terms. There are two teams here: Internacional, who at the time of our visit were world club champions (despite Stan never having heard of them before – some football fan he was then!) and Gremio, their bitter rivals from across town.

Gremio were formed by German and Italian immigrants in 1903 and thanks to a certain exclusivity inherent in their signing policy – they were made up almost entirely of German expats in their early days – they didn't even have a black player on their books until the 1950s.

Internacional, on the other hand, were formed a few years later by former residents of Sao Paulo who wanted to play football down here but were barred from joining Porto Alegre's only side. In 1909, during their first full season as a club, they lost to Gremio 10-0. Their rivals mockingly dubbed them 'monkeys'. A bitter hatred was born.

The hatred has only increased. Since then Inter have won three titles to Gremio's two and both clubs have given birth to firms ready to do anything to defend the honour of their flag. The Camisa 12, or Twelfth Shirt, of Inter and their counterparts the Geral de Gremio are notorious in this town, and derby fixtures have become twice-yearly red-letter days for the city. In the same way that certain Saturdays in the 1980s would see the city centres of

124

Liverpool, Manchester, Edinburgh and Glasgow become no-go zones for honest citizens, so a Gremio/Inter match inevitably means trouble.

Nevertheless, the atmosphere here was different to the bigger cities we had come from. All three firms we had met to this point had, in their own way, scared the shit out of us – neither of the two Porto Alegre mobs were in themselves so intimidating. In fact, if anything, we quite liked them both.

The Camisa 12 of Internacional – 'If people call us monkeys, we say we're the best looking monkeys, the strongest monkeys… we're the best fighting monkeys'

Inter had the honour of hosting their cross-town rivals the last time the two sides met: Gremio responded in suitable fashion. As the game was suspended twice and the police mounted increasingly desperate charges with tear gas and truncheons, the two firms tore into each other… and Inter's stadium took a hell of a beating.

We met Miguel, president of Camisa 12, in the back room of a bar in the shadow of their stadium. Sitting on a crate of beer surrounded by members of the firm, he explained how a clash with the police a few games before meant that the authorities were deliberately slow to act at that match.

'After a Fluminese game we battered the police,' he said, 'and this time they were too scared to jump in and separate the fighters.'

What the police had done, however, was limit the numbers allowed into the Camisa 12's terrace. Before the game even began, the home firm were outnumbered in their own manor.

The Gremio mob, out in force as you'd expect for such a match, were quick to take advantage. Heaving and pushing against the fences supposedly pinning them in, they quickly broke through and charged at the home fans, letting fly with a storm of rocks and stones as the peaceful fans they were attacking desperately tried to get out of the way.

'They tried to storm the ground from the right side of the stadium where the club members were sat, instead of coming from the left where we were,' explained Miguel. 'The club members are all old and they just sit there eating their peanuts. They don't fight anyone.'

Meanwhile, Camisa 12 were attempting a counter-charge, breaking through the Gremio lines at the other end of the stadium. The police finally acted, wading in, separating the mobs but coming under attack from both sides – and were forced time and again to retreat as firecrackers and homemade bombs spat and crackled around them. After they eventually separated the two firms, the Inter lads were forced to watch as rampant Gremio hooligans hoisted portaloos from the back of the stadium, filled them with fireworks, set fire to them and, incredibly, lobbed them down on to the pitch to burn.

The air over the Beira-Rio stadium filled with thick black smoke and the smell of burning shit, and as the fire brigade attempted to douse the flames, they too were met by a blizzard of stones and fireworks. It was not a good night for Camisa 12.

Not that these lads were about to blush or anything though. Miguel insisted that his firm were unfairly targeted by the cops that day.

'We have a lot of problems but it tends to be mainly with the military police,' he says. 'The fights in the stadium kick off because there will be an undercover cop who will start by beating someone for no apparent reason, abusing his authority. Nowadays it's quite difficult for different firms to get together. There aren't that many problems in the stadium as such but more in the metropolitan and central area of the city.'

And when the trouble starts, asked Danny, how many of you are prepared to fight?

He smiled. 'All of us – at any time and in any place.' He waved his arms around the room, indicating the lads who stood silently behind him. 'Here we teach and we learn to defend what is ours.

'I'm very proud to be here. If people call us monkeys, we say we're the best looking monkeys, the strongest monkeys… we're the best fighting monkeys. We don't have any problems being called monkeys. If someone gets left behind during a fight then we will all return to save him. You can't leave anyone behind.'

An enormous black guy in a red tracksuit, who had until that point stood with his arms folded like a bouncer behind Miguel, spoke up, his voice booming around the room. 'Football is everything,' he said, 'Inter is all about football but being in Camisa 12 means we will defend the honour of the club until the end.'

The end?

'The end,' he nodded. 'If we have to kill we will. I've been shot at. We had a disagreement with Gremio and when things got out of hand they started shooting. I got shot in the arm, but that's okay… even with guns they all still ran away.'

We left Miguel by the stadium – he asked us if we were hanging around the city for long. 'Shouldn't think so,' said Peter, brightly, 'just got one little thing to finish off and then we're gone.'

What he didn't mention was that the 'little thing' was the small matter of attending the next Gremio home game – as special guests of the Geral de Gremio.

• • •

It seemed strange to think we'd been in Brazil over a week, had met four of the country's most hardcore firms, spoken to some of the most committed football hooligans we'd met anywhere in the world, attended an all-night Samba party with boys with shooters stuck down their shorts... but still hadn't actually been to a football match. Here we were in Brazil, spiritual home of football, making a TV show about football and we hadn't seen any football.

Thankfully, that was all to change. That Sunday, Gremio were hosting our old friends Flamengo of Rio – and they were playing for a place in the Libertadores Cup, the South American equivalent of our Champions League. The stakes were high: and not only did we have tickets, we were going to be right in the thick of it, stood in the heart of the Geral de Gremio itself.

'So we're meeting Alemao, he's the top boy of the Gremio mob,' said Peter, as we got ourselves together over breakfast in the hotel. We were all buzzing with pre-match nerves but Stan had been hammering the caiparinhas the night before and had a major shake on. He assured Peter he'd be fine for filming, but it was pretty obvious he wasn't really up for covering a full-on riot.

'What's the prospects for trouble?' he asked, 'Are we going to see Paulo and the Rubro Negra boys again?'

Peter told him it was doubtful. The 2,000 mile round trip

from Rio meant that the boys from the *favelas* simply couldn't afford to come – and even if they could scrape together a coach, they'd never be able to mob up in such numbers as to make it anything other than a suicide trip.

Stan looked relieved. He needn't have done – the Geral de Gremio (literally translated: the Terrace of Gremio) were more than capable of providing enough thrills on their own.

Peter didn't really have directions to find Alemao as such. We were told to follow the crowds and Alemao would find us. As we drifted through the matchday traffic towards the ground, we noticed something different.

There were crowds alright – every corner held groups of lads laughing, singing, swapping jokes, jumpy and eager, shifting from foot to foot, eyeing the black lines of police. The streets were alive and fizzing with energy, but there was something different.

'No samba,' said Danny, suddenly. He was right. No samba, no drums, no dancing. But what there was, was drinking. Everyone had a bottle, a can, all the laughter and the singing had that alcohol-fuelled edge to it. The accents, the songs were 100 per cent Brazilian; the shorts, the bare chests, the tans and the sunshine totally South American – but the vibe itself felt... English.

Stan scratched his head. 'Am I going mad?' he asked.

'Nah mate,' muttered Danny. 'You know what this reminds me of? You're gonna think I'm off my nut, but in a funny way, this feels a bit like Upton Park on a Sunday afternoon.'

We laughed – but we did know what he meant.

Three lads appeared from nowhere and sauntered up to Peter. They were dressed identically – long shorts, bare chests, baseball caps pulled low and tattoos on their arms.

'You're looking for Alemao,' they said, and before we could answer, turned and led us down a side street.

The Geral de Gremio – 'It's my religion, it's my life, and without Gremio I am a nobody'
Alemao was waiting for us outside a bar. Tall and wiry, he too was bare-chested, but he wore his shirt like a bandana over his face, tucked into his baseball cap so all we could see were his eyes. Of all the hooligans we had met since touching down in Rio, he was the first to disguise himself.

This firm was clearly different to the rest.

'Gremio is different,' he said. 'Territorially we are part of Brazil but we are culturally separated. Our culture isn't about samba; it's a different sort of culture. The people who formed our state came from Germany, Italy, Holland and Spain – we don't have the same heritage as the rest of Brazil.'

They were also the first Brazilian crew we'd met without their own uniform. Everyone else – even the boys from the slums of Rio and Sao Paulo – managed some kind of branding, some logos, something they could wear that identified them to all comers; we still remembered the Mancha Verde's insistence that we conform to their all-green dress code.

But the Geral's lack of uniform doesn't stop them from collecting trophies from rival firms. Alemao pointed out a group of lads eager to show us their spoils of war: flags, shirts and an enormous Flamengo banner were all laid out on the pavement before them.

'A friend of mine gave me a call to say that there was a bunch of Flamengo fans at a car wash,' said one of the lads, 'so 20 of us turned up with knives, machetes, spears and guns. We told them that we weren't going to hurt them, we were only there for the banners but if they didn't give them to us we were going to kill them.' He laughed. 'And so they said we should take what we wanted.'

Nevertheless, like the top boys of just about every firm we'd met, Alemao insisted that the Geral were never the instigators of violence.

'We don't look for trouble, the trouble comes to us,' he said. 'The Gremio is the most followed and most hated firm in Brazil so the trouble comes looking for us.'

He shrugged. 'Gremio is our life. For example, if any woman wants to date me or marry me, she has to understand that today I might spend time with her but tomorrow I might be at a game, drunk and fighting whoever, police or whoever. Today, I'm at a Gremio game and I'm going to commemorate our return to the Libertadores Cup and I won't be home before tomorrow and she has to understand that. That is what the Geral is about. If Gremio is facing financial hardship, I will give the little I have to the club. It's my religion, it's my life, and without Gremio I'm a nobody.'

And that total devotion to the cause includes getting in there if it's called for. 'Everyone fights!' he shouted. 'We will never surrender; it's a life choice. In good or in evil we will fight to the end. If Gremio asked us to, we would slay a lion every day!'

'All of you?' asked Danny. 'How many of you are prepared to fight for the club?'

He made a big show of thinking. 'Hmm…let me see, how many people are going to be at the match today? 40,000? Well then I would say 35,000 would be prepared to fight.'

He laughed and slapped Danny on the back. 'And now let's go watch Gremio kick some arse, eh?'

Danny grinned. Too fucking right son. Someone handed each of us a replica shirt and a can of lager. We were going to the match.

Gremio v Flamengo – 'Wait for the Avalanche...'
The atmosphere outside the ground was nothing compared to the feeling inside. As we neared the turnstiles there was a series of 'booms' behind us and back down the street. 'Bombs,' grinned Alemao.

Inside was bedlam. Way too many people were packed into the terraces, heaving and swelling like the ocean, roaring and chanting and everyone – literally, every single person – jumping up and down in unison. It was like a human tsunami. Danny said so to Alemao.

The leader of the Geral turned and put both hands on his shoulders. 'This is nothing,' he said. 'Listen. When we score there is something called the avalanche. It would be best if you are not here for it.' Danny grinned and shook his head, but Alemao didn't smile. 'Seriously. It's not safe for you. First half you spend with us here, second half over there, with the press, where it's safe. And pray that Gremio do not score in the first half.'

Stan swallowed hard, and we followed Alemao and his henchmen as the massive sea of people parted to let us through. We scaled the terraces until we were right in the noisiest, sweatiest, most raucous part of the ground. Everyone waved a flag, a shirt, or a banner above their heads and as the teams came out we jumped and roared and kept our fists in the air with everyone else... and we kept it up for 45 minutes solid.

'Here we fucking go,' shouted Stan, 'Let's fucking have it! Let's have it now you fuckers...'

THE REAL FOOTBALL FACTORIES

It was dizzying, delirious. It was like all the lager, tequila, pills and every other drug we'd ever taken, all at once and multiplied. Being part of this delirious mob made us feel invincible, like running a marathon, like fucking a porn star, like getting on the pitch and scoring the winning goal ourselves. It was no mystery how these games descended into riots. After one half with the Geral de Gremio it seemed like Inter's stadium got off lightly with just the toilets getting burned: we felt like we could rip the place apart brick by brick.

And all of this was just while the game was progressing without incident. Nothing especially exciting was happening on the pitch – and the Geral de Gremio were jumping and roaring like every minute brought another glorious goal. And all the while we couldn't help wondering what Aleman meant about 'the avalanche' – and why he didn't think we could handle it.

Half-time came and he showed us out, parting the sea of people again like some kind of crazy Moses. 'Wait for the avalanche,' he called after us, 'and keep your cameras filming!'

We made our way round to the other end of the stadium – but if we expected the press section to be more relaxed, we were wrong again. The journalists here were rowdier than the most full-on Premiership crowds. Their notebooks and laptops were pretty much ignored as they spent the entire time on their feet, giving it everything they could.

Our throats were sore and our voices hoarse but we kept up our end – standing and singing more than we've been allowed to in England for years.

And then it happened. Ten minutes into the second half and Gremio scored. Cue chaos.

The avalanche turned out to be exactly as it sounded. Every single fan in the overcrowded end we had just come from ran full tilt at the pitch, streaming down in one insane headlong rush fast as their legs and the crush and whatever they were trampling over would allow. There was nothing at the bottom but a big fence and a concrete wall, but they flew at it for all they were worth. They hurtled down the terraces like water down stairs – like snow down a mountainside – madly, dangerously, falling and flying and surfing and stomping on each other all the way… and all to a massive animal roar that set every hair on our heads upright.

We watched them in stunned silence. 'Fuck me,' said Danny eventually. 'You do not want to be in the mix of that.'

Stan started laughing. 'Lunatics,' he cried, jumping up and down, 'total lunatics! I love it!'

Gremio scored another two after that and each time they repeated the trick – hurling themselves madly forward towards the pitch, the fences, the barriers. God knows how many got crushed each time.

Three-nil to the home side meant qualification for the Libertadores Cup and a big night for Alemao and the boys. Stan was up for finding them and joining in, but he was outvoted. We got out of there before we got caught up in it because there was still one thing left to do before we quit Brazil for good.

We were going to join the Green Stain of Sao Paulo as they journeyed to Rio for their last match of the season. It was a meaningless game – but it was going to be a far from meaningless journey.

• • •

Danny, as it turned out, had different plans. He got a call that night, he had to shoot back to London. First class, naturally, an appointment that couldn't be skipped. He'd catch up with us in Argentina.

'Nightmare, lads,' he said, with a shrug, 'nightmare. What can I say? I'll see you in a couple of days. Stay lucky, yeah?'

The rest of us travelled all night to get to the Mancha Verde in time. By 7am we were in our green t-shirts outside their headquarters again. Twenty or so members of the firm were shuffling around a knackered looking coach and we were met by Janio, who introduced us to Rafa, the resident Green Stain tattooist and the man who would be keeping an eye out for us that day. Stan asked Janio where everyone else was. Janio shrugged. We were it. Not exactly mobbed up then.

It was a six-hour journey to Rio; Palmeiras' opponents that day were to be Fluminese. The match meant nothing to either team and Janio was only leading his lads there to make a point. Not to the Fluminese fans, but to another Rio firm, the boys from Botafogo. The last time the Green Stain had come to Rio they'd been told in the clearest terms that if they returned, Botafogo would be waiting. 'They told us: "We will shoot you,"' said Janio. 'So we're coming to show we're not afraid.' Any incident today would be the third time that season that the Mancha Verde had come under fire.

'Excellent,' muttered Stan. 'We skipped a party in Porto Alegre to get shot at in Rio. Nice one.'

Nevertheless, we settled in with the other lads and after we hit the freeway and a few breakfast beers had been cracked open, everyone relaxed a little. Rafa explained how the Mancha Verde had become his whole life: now in his late

30s, he'd even skipped his own sister's wedding for his firm – missing the marriage to catch Palmeiras in a pre-season friendly. 'She was very upset,' he laughed.

She was not the only one. Rafa's wife asked him to choose between the firm and his family: he chose the Mancha Verde and she left, taking his daughter with her. 'She was scared,' he said. 'It's hard. I suffer… but Mancha runs in my veins.' He showed us tattoos he had drawn on himself– Isadora, the name of his daughter, was a recurring motif.

By the time we got to Rio we knew Rafa's whole life story. Stan promised him that when we got back to England he would have a Palmeiras tattoo done in honour of him.

The game itself passed without incident. The players were as lacklustre as most of the fans, and although our boys kept their end up, there was a jumpiness in the air. We all knew that while we were here watching the game, the word was out in the city that we had arrived. As we were led back to our bus by a handful of armed police, Janio explained how they would provide us with an escort out of Rio. 'We're safe to the city limits,' he said. 'And then… who knows?'

The mood was tense and as we pulled on to the freeway the atmosphere grew. The coach was silent, the curtains drawn and behind them faces peered out nervously at each passing car. Stan slipped in the seat next to Rafa, who was keeping his eyes on the road.

'Not long now,' he said, pointing at our escort. We'd made Rio city limits. The police car was indicating; as the junction approached it pulled off and we were on our own.

The driver put his foot down, pulled into the outside lane. It was a straight road from here to Sao Paulo, but we were in bandit country and any one of the other cars on the freeway could be loaded with Botafogo. Rafa reckoned it would be four hours before we could relax. Up and down the coach, pistols were drawn. Stan turned his camera on.

It took less than 15 minutes for the tension to break. Stan was sweating hard and he leaned forward to retrieve an unopened can of beer that was rolling on the floor. As he bent over the window behind him exploded. The window next to Rafa's head. Three loud cracks and then tiny shards of glass everywhere. It all seemed to happen in slow motion. Stan raised his head in confusion just as Rafa fell forward on to him. Several other people hit the deck – the rest ran to the windows, guns out.

'They've shot my fucking window!' yelled Rafa, over and over. 'They've shot my fucking window!'

'The windows,' repeated Stan, slowly, raising his head and staring stupidly at the shattered glass immediately to the right of where he and Rafa had been sitting a few seconds before. 'They've shot the windows.'

Some of the boys were leaning out of the coach, shouting and waving their weapons at a car behind; the driver kept his foot hard down and we careered along the road at breakneck speed. The car with the gunmen in eased off the gas and we pulled away.

'They shot the windows,' Stan kept repeating, like he couldn't believe it. He held up the camera, still filming, to take in the broken glass, the torn curtains, the scattered men and the unmistakeable look of fear on the face of Rafa as he crouched next to him.

'The bullet passed behind me,' he said, grabbing Stan's camera and speaking into the lens. 'This close. This close to death, Stan; I was this close to death.' He let go, leaned forward again and buried his head in his hands. On his arm one tattooed word stood out: Isadora.

CHAPTER SIX

ARGENTINA

Talk about timing. Our arrival in the land of Maradona and Las Malvinas coincided with the biggest crisis in the history of Argentinian football violence. We flew straight into the eye of an almighty storm and, as it all kicked off around us, we even became part of the story ourselves.

We were at the last game before away fans were banned from the terraces for the rest of the season – Independiente v Racing. As the match was abandoned and football forgotten in favour of a full-on riot, we became part of a whole new war on hooliganism.

In the firms we met here we saw something we didn't encounter anywhere else in the world. And it wasn't what we were expecting.

'Buenos Aries,' shouted Danny, as our taxi took us through streets gleaming in the morning sunshine, beautiful buildings and beautiful people everywhere we looked, the whole place humming and vibrant and alive with colour and energy. 'Buenos Aries, watch out! The English are here!'

Stan laughed. Peter grinned. The taxi driver had a face like stone.

It didn't deter us. None of us had been to Argentina before and its capital is a beautiful city. We were 7,000 miles from London, we were over halfway through our round-the-world trip, the sun was shining, the girls were gorgeous and we were looking forward to meeting boys whose passion for the beautiful game was matched only by their handiness on the terraces.

What was not to be happy about?

We were always going to come to Argentina. There's the traditional rivalry between them and us, of course, we couldn't ignore that – Beckham in 98, Maradona in 86, Port Stanley in 82. But then there's also Ossie Ardiles, Ricky Villa, Carlos Tevez – boys from the Barrios – who have, one way or another, made a major impact on our leagues.

Love it or hate it, somehow the English and Argentine games are inextricably connected. It's always been the case. A football league was established here by British immigrants way back in 1891, just three years after our own was formed – and before any in mainland Europe.

And as every Englishman knows with a lurch in his heart, fixtures between the two countries never fail to provide drama, excitement and the kind of intensity you only normally get at derby games.

This, after all, is the home of Diego Maradona. One of the greatest players to ever grace the pitch, scorer of some of the most sublime goals the game has ever seen, genius, inspiration, drug addict, cheat. He's the man who in the space of four minutes in 1986 scored the most infamous goal in World Cup history, followed by arguably the greatest goal in World Cup history.

Part angel, part devil, Maradona's contradictions reflect the country itself. And we were going to meet one of his friends – a man who also happens to be the leader of the most notorious firm in Buenos Aries.

There are two great passions in Argentina. Football is one of them. Violence is the other. Even more so than its larger and more successful neighbour Brazil, the country lives and breathes football. They play the game with a unique combination of European grit and South American flair – and they support football with a fervour unlike anywhere else on the planet.

And if Argentina is a country unrivalled in its passion for football, its capital is where that passion is most volatile. Buenos Aries has the greatest concentration of football teams of any city in the world, and no less than 10 of them are in the country's top flight.

A lot of football teams means a lot of firms. And that means a lot of trouble. This is a society built on bloodshed; its recent history is a litany of brutality.

In 1943 a military coup paved the way for four decades of regimes who ruled through fear and intimidation. There were kidnaps and assassinations, newspapers were harassed and shut down, voices opposed to the authorities suddenly silenced. Human rights groups reckon that between 1976 and 1983 alone, some 30,000 Argentines 'disappeared' speaking up against the government. No one knows what has happened to them.

Violence is endemic here: it's part of the culture.

And naturally, if you take that and you throw their passion for football in the mix, you've got an explosive combination.

141

Since 1939 there have been over 220 official victims of football violence in Argentina – the real number of dead is thought to be far higher.

The first trouble occurred as far back as 1916: while we were playing the pipes of peace and knocking a ball about with the Germans at the Somme, in South America they were at war on the pitch, and a match between Argentina and Uruguay had to be called off due to 'violent incidents' on the terraces. The first football hooligan fatalities came in 1939, during a Boca v Lanus game. A foul escalated into a bit of pushing and shoving – which then escalated further when some of the Lanus fans joined in. This sparked mayhem on the Boca stands. They streamed down the terraces to get stuck in themselves and a policemen panicked and fired towards the crowd. Two supporters were hit, both died.

In the late 1950s supporters' groups began to get properly organized. Known as the 'Barras Bravas' or 'Brave Gangs', they now dominate football support here. As we would discover, their influence extends way beyond organizing weekend tear-ups.

And it's not just the supporters who like a ruck. Stan had a book of football trivia and he read out the section on the peculiarities of Argentinian on-pitch discipline. They made the Arsenal/Man U spats look pretty lame, to say the least.

In the 1966 World Cup a referee was assaulted in the tunnel and the Argentine team tried to storm the English dressing room after we beat them 1-0 in the quarter-finals. The furious players had to be held back by the police and stewards.

A year later when Racing Club played Celtic for the World Club Championship six were sent off and armed police were on the pitch within half an hour of kick off. The last to be dismissed was Bertie Auld, who refused to leave the field. So the ref let him play on.

If six dismissals sounds like a farce, in 1971 Boca Juniors v Sporting Cristal of Peru took a lack of discipline to the extremes. No less than 19 players were sent off – and then arrested – as the match descended into a full-on brawl.

Stan grinned. 'Nineteen sent off! Fucking loco man! What a country! Love it!'

If Stan had been at all affected by getting shot at in Brazil, he wasn't showing it. Far from losing his bottle for the job, if anything he was more excited than before.

'Can't wait to meet these crazy fuckers,' he said. 'Bring it on. Bring it all on!'

The Red Devils of Independiente – 'The violence is in Argentina. The violence is in society. From there it goes on to the football pitch…'

If our normal routine was to travel around a country meeting different firms, it didn't really make sense to do that here. With all the big players based in Buenos Aries we figured we'd stay put. And apart from anything else, we were knackered. It was going to be good to spend more than two nights in the same bed.

The other difference was that this time we were going to watch a game before we did pretty much anything else. Our boys had fixed it for us to catch up with the top man of the Red Devils of Independiente – and he was going to take us to that weekend's biggest, nastiest show in town: Independiente v Racing Club. We were going to be right among the Red Devils, packed into their specially reserved section of the terraces.

As it turns out, we weren't going to last that long.

We had arranged to meet Pablo Alavarez – known as 'Bebote' or the Big Baby – top boy of the Red Devils at Independiente's ground at midday. Kick off wasn't until four, but he said that getting there early was essential. He was a busy man; he had things to do.

There wasn't a cloud in the sky and we were already sweltering when we pulled up outside Independiente's Estadio Libertadores de America – a grand name for an ancient, crumbling concrete monstrosity. Built in 1928 and with a capacity of about 50,000, it's the kind of stadium you just don't see in Europe anymore – all massive concrete terraces and high fences topped with barbed wire. Between the stands and the pitch there was a moat in which what looked like raw sewage floated. No one was going to be invading the pitch here.

We were greeted by Bebote with a smile and a handshake and he handed us each a bin bag. 'Come on,' he said, 'we have work to do.'

As we hauled the bags after him, Peter asked Danny what he thought they might contain.

'Knives,' he whispered. 'Machetes.'

Stan stopped. 'No way!' and split his open for a better look. It was full of balloons. On each was written a 'No to Violence!' message. If Stan looked disappointed, Peter started laughing. It was to be just the first of a series of very strange contradictions from Bebote.

Independiente are known as 'El Rey de Copas' (The King of Cups), because they have won 15 international trophies, including the Copa Libertadores seven times – more than any other club in South America. And their firm, the Red Devils, has accordingly built up a reputation to match.

Not that you'd think it from Bebote's description of their activities.

'What the Barras does is to cheer and organize,' he said. 'As you've seen we've got plenty of balloons and plenty of flags... We arrive early because we need to distribute the balloons. There will be almost 50,000 people here today so we need to distribute the balloons, get the flags organized and cheer for the team throughout the whole game.'

Stan and Peter exchanged glances. Peter asked how many of the 50,000 could claim to be part of Bebote's Barras – and for how long they've been organized.

'There are around 500 of us,' he shrugged. 'And I've been coming here for the last 20 years and they already existed then, so I'd say the Red Devils have been here for the last 100 years. In 1997 I took over the firm leadership. My job is to make sure the lads behave.'

'Is there a lot of violence at the game?' asked Danny.

Bebote grinned. 'No, no!' he said. 'The violence is in Argentina and not in football. The violence is in society. From there it goes on to the football pitch, to the dance, it's in all parts of the society. We'll try to make sure nothing happens here today but the violence could be anywhere.

'Of course, when it comes to self-defence we're all ready to defend ourselves. We're not here to look for trouble but if we need to defend ourselves then we're all ready for it, like anyone else. Like yourself,' and he motioned to Stan, 'if you're attacked, you defend yourself, right?'

Stan gave no reaction.

'How many of you?' asked Danny. 'If one of you was attacked – how many of you would defend him? All 500 of you?'

'Well, if one of the 500 isn't up for it, he'll surely have trouble with me,' he said.

Bebote's phone rang and he wandered off. We looked at each other.

'What do you think?' asked Danny.

'I think he's got a pretty bad memory, for one thing,' said Peter.

Bebote's firm are not exactly all about balloons and saying no to violence and only reacting when provoked – in fact their history since Bebote took over as top man would seem to suggest the exact opposite.

In March 1997 the start of the Independiente v Racing derby was delayed after a knife was thrown from the Red Devils end, landing near the opposition's goalmouth. As tensions grew fights broke out between sets of supporters in and outside the ground.

Three months later at a match between Racing and River Plate, Waldo Rodriguez, a member of Racing's firm Racing Stone, was killed. Fans of Independiente were fingered for the crime.

In April 1999 Racing and Gimnasia hooligans got together for a supposedly peaceful protest against a referee that had halted a Racing match... The Red Devils ambushed both firms and in the resulting trouble seven people were seriously injured and one shot at.

Early the next season the build up to the Independiente–Racing derby was even more heated: in extended fighting before and after the match 27 were arrested, seven hospitalized and one fan treated for bullet wounds.

The following year's derby saw over 100 people injured and later that season after a Racing–Belgrano game, a Racing fan was killed after being stabbed 17 times. Independiente firm members were accused of the murder.

In February 2002 this fixture sparked a major riot in the Avallaneda district both clubs share. It began with disturbances at the train station and further trouble escalated around the ground, before, during and after the game. The police waded in, shots were fired. Hundreds were injured and 25 arrested – and it remains a mystery how no one was killed.

'So what's with all the "our job is to blow up balloons and organize songs" stuff?' asked Danny. 'You know what it is? It's sinister. Balaclavas and blades I can understand. Fronting up, telling us how bad they are I can understand. But this?'

'And, you know, every firm we've met – they've all been about bravado, violence, being dangerous, being naughty. And here we've got these geezers, one of the naughtiest firms in South America... and their top boy is telling us how gentle they are!' He shivered. 'It gives me the willies, I don't mind telling you.'

It was going to get worse. Bebote was taking us into the thick of it, the specially reserved section of the Red Devils end, in the heart of the terrace where even the police don't go.

Independiente v Racing Club – 'Well. Out. Me. Manor.'
The atmosphere was insane. Like hell. No booze, no drugs... but every single person crammed in there jumping and shouting and dancing and singing and off their faces on adrenaline or something.

The intensity was unbelievable. We'd been in the thick of some serious mobs, but nothing like this. The noise was a constant roar, the concrete terraces shook – literally, shook – with the impact of thousands of men jumping and stamping their feet. Bebote's balloons were everywhere – along with banners, flags, effigies. People were dressed as devils, people were running crazily up and down the stands, people were balanced on each other's shoulders, people were just standing there screaming at the top of their voices... it was bedlam.

'This is lawless,' shouted Stan, 'It's fucking lawless is what it is. Anything could happen.'

Danny grabbed Stan's shirt. 'Look at them,' he shouted, 'Look at their eyes – all this passion and venom in their eyes. I can see it man. I tell you what, I feel well out me manor. Well. Out. Me. Manor.'

Someone came running past and leapfrogged clean over Danny, using Stan's shoulders as leverage. 'And another thing,' he shouted. 'This is the first time that I've gone into a firm and they haven't seen *The Football Factory*. They know nothing about me. I can't rely on anything here, me boat, I'm just some English cockney twat to them. I feel about that big, and that's no word of a lie.'

'Just keep jumping,' shouted Stan, 'keep fucking jumping and we might be okay...'

The noise was so massive that we didn't even notice when the game kicked off. Not until Stan pointed out the Racing fans on the opposing terraces – they were keeping their end up, jumping and shaking the separating fences. They looked to be pretty well mobbed up too – in the hundreds at least.

Suddenly it went quiet.

'Oh shit,' whispered Stan. 'We've got a penalty.'

As the Independiente number 11 stroked it in the whole place erupted. It was like a bomb going off smack in the middle of us – everyone ran forwards, bodies scattered everywhere, flags and flares and balloons and shirts and people thrown into the air and a roar like a tidal wave deafening in our ears. It was like drowning, being electrocuted, being kicked to death and being at the best rave you've ever heard about... all at the same time. In Spanish. Surrounded by Argentinian football hooligans. Dressed as devils.

'I think I've shit my pants!' yelled Danny as Stan went hurtling past him, carried on the surge way down the terraces towards the fences and the barbed wire.

Bebote appeared from nowhere. 'I think it's time you left,' he said. 'I don't think it's going to be safe for you any more.'

'No fucking arguments here son,' said Danny, grabbing him like a drowning man grabs a life ring. He led us out of the stands and towards the relatively subdued supporters in the press area... and then went back into the chaos for Stan.

As we regrouped, Stan was shaking. 'Fucking amazing,' was all he could say. 'Fucking amazing.'

We'd barely lasted 10 minutes of the match with the Red Devils.

As it turned out, Bebote got us out at the right time. In the second half another goal for the home side became the catalyst for the Racing mob to show what they were made of.

At first it all went quiet over there. All the singing, all the movement stopped. It was like a big intake of breath...

And then a single stone went arcing across the fences. And then another. And then the air was full of them, a hard rain of rocks and bricks and bits of concrete, showering the exact place we'd been 45 minutes before.

The stones were followed by a charge against the fencing and the line of police that stood there. Sticks were chucked, flagpoles were thrown like javelins, it even looked like lumps of the stadium itself were being volleyed towards the police.

The authorities weren't going to stand and take it. We watched as they fired tear gas into the surging crowds – and then groaned as the clouds drifted across the pitch and the referee suspended the match.

The ref's whistle was like a signal. The violence snowballed – wave after wave of the Racing mob charged the black lines of police, the noise of their attacks punctuated by muffled booms as smoke bombs exploded and smaller cracks and pops of what we hoped were fireworks.

The police were losing control – and so they brought out their hoses. One half of the stadium descended into a mess of water and tear gas and smoke and rubble as they launched their counter attacks... and the referee had seen enough. He blew again; the match was abandoned.

'Fucking hell,' muttered Danny, as we left them to it. Even as we escaped the stadium we could hear the riot continuing. They would be at it for a few more hours yet – and this was all before Bebote's lads could get at them. Christ knows what was going to happen then.

● ● ●

The next morning we met for breakfast. Stan got the coffees in as one of our contacts out here laid out the newspapers and filled us in. It seemed that our riot had been the last straw. The headline in one of the biggest-selling papers Ole said it all: 'The war on violence has begun'.

As of that morning the Argentine FA had had enough. Our match had kicked them into action. It seemed that the Racing firm's tactics of deliberately starting a riot to get a match abandoned – and thus save them the humiliation of a defeat

– were a step too far for the authorities. For the last four games of the season away fans were to be banned – and any team whose fans caused trouble were to have points deducted.

We'd arrived at exactly the right time. It seemed that yesterday's trouble was typical of the way football over here was going.

As we read on, the full scale of the problem began to become apparent. The month before our arrival had seen Buenos Aries become a battlefield – but what made these incidents stand out from others we'd seen around the world was that the trouble wasn't just confined to the lads on the terraces. Here it seems football violence goes all the way to the top.

In the preceding four weeks Racing Club had banned members of the Boca Juniors firm known as La Doce or 'The Twelfth Shirt' from coming into the ground. When a judge overturned the ban as unlawful, Racing called the game off saying that they could not provide adequate security.

Then Indepediente banned the hooligans of River Plate from attending their stadium for the match.

During a game between Newell's Old Boys and Rosario Central police fired rubber bullets at rioting Newell's fans at half-time. Even the players got involved with that one – some got into trouble for trying to stop the police from firing into the crowds.

And as if all that wasn't enough, a referee accused the club president of Gimnasia La Plata of behaving like a hooligan and physically threatening him in the locker room at half-time. The ref suspended the match.

The Gimnasia firm then allegedly burst into their own players' dressing room with guns and threatened their own team with death if they won the game – a Gimnasia win would have helped their bitter rivals Estudiantes in the league.

'Hang on,' said Danny, 'I can't quite get my nut around that one. They said they'd kill them if they won?'

Our man shrugged. 'This is Argentina,' he said. 'This is passion.' According to him, football support here followed a strict gang mentality. Your team isn't just something you follow – they are representatives of your neighbourhood. And the firm are defenders of that neighbourhood. All victories, all humiliations reflect directly back on your manor.

It was the same in every paper – and when we turned on the TV it was on every channel. We'd flown into the eye of a hooligan storm.

'All this is great,' said Peter. 'Except we're never going to get anyone to talk to us now, are we?'

Our contact grinned. 'You don't understand,' he said. 'This is not Europe. Our firms don't care about a few words in the media. It's all hot air. Talking loud, saying nothing.'

He'd already set up a meeting for later that day with a firm called the Pandilla (which is simply another word for 'gang') of Velez Sarsfield – and if we were lucky, the next day we'd be having dinner with a man called Rafa Di Zeo. We'd never heard of him – but we were about the only people south of the Rio Grande who hadn't. Top boy of La Doce of Boca Juniors, he's also the most notorious football hooligan in Argentina.

'Business as usual,' grinned our man.

The Pandilla of Velez Sarsfield – 'Refreshments, sir?'
Argentina just kept getting more and more surreal. Our interview with the boys from Velez Sarsfield was to be so

unrevealing as to be almost unusable... but if what they said told us nothing, everything else about our encounter spoke volumes.

Velez Sarsfield is based in the most westerly barrio of Buenos Aries, right on the edge of town... and if they weren't a club familiar to any of us, that was more to do with our ignorance than their lack of talent. They've got an impressively packed trophy cabinet – and in 1994 they even beat the then all-conquering AC Milan to win the world club cup.

Their ground is pretty tasty, too – built up on all sides, it's like a cauldron, holding the atmosphere in. We were shown through the gates and introduced to Ezequiel, who runs their firm: we could imagine both players and rival mobs getting intimidated by the place.

As Ezequiel took us on a guided tour of the stadium, we didn't actually realize just who he was. As he talked us through the trophies, the history; as he walked us through the dressing rooms, the boardrooms, we thought he was some kind of club official. It was only when he invited us back on to the pitch to meet the other lads in his firm that we twigged.

And it didn't make sense. Ezequiel was a hooligan. He was the top man in the Pandilla... he was the one responsible for kicking lumps out of all the other firms, the one supposedly sorting out riots and set-tos with the police. He was the one who, according to that morning's papers, his club had just declared war on. And yet he'd just shown us around the Velez Sarsfield boardroom! Nobody had asked what we were doing in there, nobody had called security, nobody had served us with banning orders...

What the fuck?

It got madder. Ezequiel was just explaining how in his

crew of 300 or so boys (there were maybe seven of them there today, and if they weren't exactly being treated like hooligans, they at least looked the part: tattoos, baseball caps pulled low, the swagger and the hard eyes) they all enjoyed getting stuck in there.

'The fights here are not organized,' he said. 'They're spontaneous. But if you bump into someone from another firm, you do fight. There is no other way. We prefer to fight with another firm, not with the police... if we fight the police, we lose. Things are much more controlled now and the police are much better organized.

'The police reaction to trouble is often too much and it's not justified. They'll just start off against innocent people for no reason. They see a stone coming down and they counter-attack right away. They don't think about the women, children, old people in the seated area of the terraces who are not fit enough to take this. There are sometimes babies around...'

Peter's attention was distracted. 'Hold up a sec, lads,' he said, looking past Danny and Ezequiel as a man in a suit and bow tie walked straight across the pitch towards us. He was carrying a tray of bottles.

Stan kept the camera on him. 'If we weren't on a football pitch with a gang of hooligans talking about fighting the police... I'd say that was a waiter,' he said. 'A waiter sent out by the club's management to make sure we didn't get too thirsty. But obviously as we are with a gang of hooligans talking about fighting the police, I must be seeing things, right?'

The man approached us with a big smile on his face, bowed to Ezequiel and started handing out ice-cold bottles of lager. 'Refreshments, sir?' he beamed at Danny.

'Uh, yeah, nice one,' said Danny. 'Um. Cheers then.'

The Pandilla all clinked bottles.

'They've got their own butler,' muttered Stan. 'They're the only firm in the world with their own butler.' He took a bottle himself. 'Fucking loco, man...'

It was all a bit much. The guided tour, the easy access to all corners of the stadium, the casual use of the pitch as an interview location – can you imagine talking to known hooligans on Old Trafford's turf? Or Chelsea's? Or even Dagenham & Redbridge's? No chance! – it was almost like the Pandilla are considered men of some influence at Velez Sarsfield football club. Like they're not only tolerated – but actually respected. Like they're an integral part of the organization.

And now, to top it all, the cherry on the cake... the club have provided their firm with a butler. Because, you know, it's thirsty work explaining to English TV crews how you like to kick the shit out of other football supporters.

Stan had it right. Fucking loco. The lunatics were taking over the asylum.

• • •

We came out of our chat with the Pandilla straight into another gobsmacker. It turned out that while we'd been chewing the fat with that firm, our man Bebote – the same man who had got us into (and then got us out of) the heart of the Red Devils end at the Independiente v Racing game; the same man who had got to the ground four hours before kick off to sort out balloons and banners; the same man who had told us 'my job is to make sure the lads behave'... he was only all over the news. As a wanted man.

Bebote, it seems, was actually banned from the game he took us to. And the governor of Buenos Aries himself was alleging that the Independiente club president knew that Bebote was at the match – and that he'd let him in early deliberately. And on top of all that, he'd also accused our man of selling 600 illegal tickets for the game!

It turned out that football firms in this country were very different beasts than they are in Europe. We'd already guessed that a little bit... but the full extent of just how different was only now beginning to dawn on us.

In Argentina, football clubs are run like Associations, not companies like we're used to. The club president isn't appointed by a board of suits... he's voted for. And that means, if you want to be president, you need the backing of the terraces.

And it also means that if you control the terraces, you can control the president.

The Barras Bravas do control the terraces. Firms like the Red Devils and the Pandilla and La Doce of Boca Juniors – they are the heartbeat of support for their clubs... and top boys like Bebote wield massive influence on what the rank and file supporters think and do.

No wonder they were all being so cagy. It's been alleged that in Argentina, far from the football clubs trying to distance themselves from the firms, they're actually enjoying a close relationship with them...

It takes hooliganism here to a different level altogether. It makes firms here not just a bunch of lads who like to kick off at the weekend – but a set of seriously organized criminal gangs, practising extortion, intimidation and corruption.

Now none of us were about to jump to any conclusions, but given the weird morning we'd just spent at Velez Sarsfield, it did look like there might be something in this theory of Argentine football firms as a kind of sophisticated criminal organization, a mafia.

It also meant that this so-called declaration of war on the hooligans really was, as our man here had said, nothing but hot air.

Peter called a meeting. Things were going pear-shaped. He wanted to talk to the police, get the official line on things. Make like proper journalists.

The only problem was... the police didn't want to talk to us. Peter spent an hour with them trying to persuade them... but to no avail. Normally when the authorities won't meet us it's because they think we're glamourising the violence, encouraging the firms. Here they were keeping schtum because they considered the situation too dangerous, too volatile. They were frightened of what would happen.

'The police,' repeated Peter, 'are frightened of repercussions. Whatever that means.'

There was another problem. The governor of Buenos Aries – the same man who had called for the head of Bebote – had been a very busy boy it seemed. He'd been on the radio again, and this time he'd been talking about us. He wanted to know what we were doing here, he'd suggested we were inflaming the situation, he said he wanted to see our footage... 'and worst of all, he said we were from the BBC,' said Peter. 'The BBC... Doesn't half wind me up.'

'So we've become part of the story,' said Danny. 'And now I'm guessing no one's going to talk to us, right?'

Peter brightened. He'd made a call. And we still had Rafa Di Zeo. 'Only the top boy of the biggest firm in Argentina,' he grinned.

La Doce of Boca Juniors – 'We represent the club. We're here from our childhood till our death...'

Rafa Di Zeo, as it turned out, is not your average football hooligan. For a start he's 45 years old, married, intelligent, charming. He's a celebrity in this country – the camera picks him out at games, he features on the cover of magazines, it's even said he has the ears of some of the most powerful men in the country. Oh – and Diego Maradona is a close personal friend.

He also controls La Doce – or The Twelfth Shirt – Boca Juniors' notorious hooligan army of some 2,000 boys strong.

La Doce have been involved in some of the worst violence seen in world football. In the mid 90s, after Boca had lost 2-0 to bitter rivals River Plate, two River fans were shot dead. La Doce of course denied involvement... but around the city the following graffiti appeared: 'River 2-2 Boca'.

In 2002 the return fixture was abandoned and once again a fan was found shot dead.

They've also flexed their muscles in the boardrooms and dressing rooms of the club. It was La Doce who, back in 1981, pressurized the club's authorities into making Maradona captain of the team. And it's said that they used their power to influence the club's buying and selling policy to support him.

Maradona never forgot it – and has become a public and outspoken friend of Rafa and his crew. 'My relationship with the guys is excellent,' the Argentine legend said recently. 'We get together through their songs, through the passion for the colours of our team... then they go and make their mistakes and I do mine, we certainly don't enter into an association of crime, that's not my style.'

For their part, La Doce is equally forgiving of their idol. 'We never turned our backs on him like the media,' Rafa told us. 'When they were proud of him they'd treat him well and when they disliked him they'd treat him badly. We've always treated him well. He's always been our friend and we've always been his. In fact, he even came to my wedding.'

But naturally it's not all backslaps with Boca legends. Rafa himself may be a public figure here – and a hero to thousands of fervent young Boca fans – but he's also attracted interest of another kind.

In 1999, Boca Juniors played Chacarita. There was massed fighting outside the ground before the game and two Chacarita fans ended up dead.

In 2003, the two sides were due to meet again and the game had to be called off after plans were uncovered to stage a rematch of the fight outside Chacarita's ground before the match.

The police had been trying to catch up with Rafa ever since. Although at the time we were there he was still officially innocent-until-proven-guilty, it was pretty common knowledge that he'd been fingered as having a part to play in the 1999 murders.

It was a strange situation. Rafa Di Zeo was probably the most famous person we were going to meet this whole trip. And he was also a wanted man. And we were about to have dinner with him.

Peter had been told that we were to wait in a petrol station near the Boca region of the city – someone would be along to meet us. It was like being back in Eastern Europe again, all the cloak and dagger stuff. Only this time, as it turned out, Danny actually had a dagger.

'What the fuck is that?' demanded Peter, as Danny unsheathed six inches of shining steel for the camera. Stan zoomed in on it, eyes bright.

'Look at who I'm with,' said Danny. 'No offence, you're nice guys – but could you hold your hands up when it all goes off? Where's the security? And this Rafa's a serious bloke we're meeting. This is not just a little bit of Argy Bargy on the terraces, you know. This is getting deep. I've had to take matters into me own hands. I want you to say hello to my little friend.'

Stan started laughing. Peter kept frowning.

'Now, you know, I've got kids, I've got an old woman, I've got to look after me self,' continued Danny, winking at the camera. 'Now, I don't want to... believe me, the last thing I wanna do is to start swinging this about at people, you know? It's just for a bit of peace of mind, si? Just for my peace of mind, you know what I mean? It's a nice little... what?'

Peter was staring out of the window. A man dressed all in black was approaching.

'Jesus!' spluttered Danny, stuffing the blade down the back of his seat. 'They've just turned up and I've got this in me hand...'

Stan took the knife off him and put it in his own pocket.

'Cheers pal,' said Danny.

'No problem,' replied Stan, as the door opened and the man got in, shook hands with Peter and started the car. 'No problem at all.'

We were driven to a pizza restaurant. The whole thing was becoming like a scene from *The Godfather* – and when we were introduced to Rafa Di Zeo it didn't get any less Mafia-like. Dressed casually and with a shock of white hair, he sat with his back to the wall and in a spot where he could see the whole restaurant. Around him were blank-faced geezers with their hands in their pockets. At least one person was always on the phone. Two more stood at the door to the pizzeria.

Were we intimidated? We were shitting ourselves.

As usual, Danny's tactic was to front his way through his nerves. Giving it the full eye contact, he extended his hand to the Boca top man. 'Pleased to meet you,' he said, 'Real pleasure.' He winked at his henchmen. 'Alright lads? How's the garlic bread, alright? Sweet, looks tasty...'

'Okay,' interrupted Peter, 'So Rafa, I thought maybe we could ask a few questions about La Doce...'

Rafa shrugged. 'Sure, whatever.'

'Great! Um. Ok. So perhaps first you could tell us how someone becomes a member of La Doce?'

'Ok,' he said. 'You can come with someone who's already a member who can vouch for you. Some people get involved in fights without being recognized by us and if they prove to be valuable they can then join us that way. There are also other ways, for example if someone does something that's beneficial for Boca it opens his door to La Doce...'

Danny asked him what the role of La Doce actually was.

'At the club it's like one of its strong legs,' he said. 'Think about it. Players come to a club because the club buys them. They come for a certain time. The club management, the president and so on, are elected for a four-year period... but the fan, La Doce, is there all his life. So if we look at the timeframe we've got much more influence in the club. We represent the club. We're here from our childhood till our death...

'La Doce is the largest club representative there is. And we always represent the club. I remember once Boca lost 3-0 and everyone left the terraces... only the 2,000 of us were left. In La Doce no one leaves till I leave.'

Finally, it felt like we were getting somewhere. Rafa might have been an intimidating bloke – but at least our chat wasn't being interrupted by balloon blowing or club butlers. Peter tried to steer him round to specific incidents involving his firm's more violent side.

The atmosphere changed immediately. Rafa was silent for a minute. 'These are not nice things to talk about and one tends not to talk about them,' he said, quietly.

'It does happen though, eh?' said Stan, as both Peter and Danny turned to stare at him like he was mad. 'You do fight, don't you?'

Rafa looked Stan up and down. 'The fights are something from the past and they stay in the past,' he said. 'We don't talk about the subject a lot. We know we've had a fight and we tend to comment if we've won or lost – we usually win, by the way – but that's all. We don't really go into any further details about the fights.'

Peter kept his eye on Stan as Danny tried to talk him round. 'In England hooligans that we've met like to boast about the violence, they are quite proud of it. In Argentina they are less open. Why do you think this is?' he asked, as behind him Stan shrugged at Peter.

'It's more closed because our world is more closed,' replied Rafa. 'We don't want our things to get public. That's why it's more closed and that's why people don't want to talk a lot.

'I talk on behalf of the Boca fans and we are like a family. So what we try to do is to keep family problems within the family. Do you understand that?'

He flicked his eyes at someone behind us and suddenly our driver reappeared. It seemed our interview was over – and before we'd even had a chance to try a pizza ourselves.

'Just before we go,' said Peter, 'what do you think about the anti-hooligan measures they're putting into place now... banning away fans and threatening to dock points? Do you think it will help to stop the trouble?'

Rafa waved his hand dismissively. 'This is a temporary thing. We are right at the end of our league and it'll only affect the last four games. You can't ask people not to go to away games. It doesn't make any sense.

'What are the police there for, what are the security organizations there for if no one is to enter the game? There are people in the club that live on the income from this as well as the security people and many others so they can't do it, can they? And they can't ask a fan of a club not to support his team on away games, can they?'

He shrugged. 'I'm not worried about it at all.'

And that was it. Interview over. We were shown the door.

We'd got just about all we were going to get from Argentina – and to be fair, in less than a week we'd seen a match abandoned, narrowly escaped a riot, got caught up in Argentina's biggest ever crackdown on football violence, been declared wanted by the governor of Buenos Aries and met the man who could justifiably call himself the biggest name in world hooliganism.

And it was all so different from the kind of stuff we were used to. The firms over here were like the mafia, a secret and powerful world. They weren't about fronting up, making a show... they were about closing ranks and hiding what really goes on. It wasn't as in-your-face terrifying as some of the places we'd been... but it was miles more intense.

We left Argentina with the governor still talking about trying to catch up with us. Even as we left he was still banging on about the BBC crew with the behind-the-scenes hooligan coverage.

'Fucking BBC,' said Stan. 'Silly old sod.'

A few months later we got a call: the police had finally caught up with Rafa Di Zeo. In March 2007, in a court in Buenos Aries, the head of La Doce was sentenced for four and a half years in jail for his part in the 1999 Chacarita deaths.

CHAPTER SEVEN

RUSSIA

Russia's got a brutal past – and for some it's an equally painful present. From communism to capitalism, Russia has embraced ideological extremes – and its hooligans are exploiting these new freedoms for their own vicious ends. Moscow has become a battlefield in a war of supremacy between the country's nastiest mobs – men and boys with nothing but their fists and their thick skins to show their love for teams now bankrolled by billionaires. And in the nation's former capital of St Petersburg lurks Mother Russia's new hooligan order: a firm put together as a crack fighting unit specifically to take on the big boys of Europe.

They don't mess about here. They're hardcore. And in this massive country of massive contrasts, the strangest thing of all is that sometimes it's the hooligans themselves imposing some kind of order on a society spinning out of control.

'It's the unknown that excites me,' said Danny, as we stood in Red Square staring up at the bulbs and domes and fairytale turrets of the Kremlin. Our breath billowed in clouds around us, our skin was goose bumped and turning blue from cold. 'I know nothing about Russia. Absolutely nothing.' He fumbled to get a cigarette out of the packet, before giving up. 'Other than it's fucking freezing. Too cold to smoke. Warsaw was cold but this... this rips through your bones.'

Everyone nodded. Around us people hurried through the huge concrete expanse, shoulders hunched against the bitter air – and, it seemed, hunched against the weight of the government buildings surrounding them, against the weight of all their history and bloodshed.

'Let's get a vodka,' said Peter, 'and I'll take you to a man who can give us a crash course on Russian hooligan history.'

Moscow today is a very different place from how it was during the heyday of British hooliganism. Before the break-up of the Soviet Union in 1991, it wasn't easy being a football fan here. Under communist rule individuality was crushed – and if that meant that speaking up against the powers-that-be wasn't allowed, it also meant that demonstrations of any kind were banned. Including demonstrations of football support.

The big clubs – Spartak Moscow, CSKA Moscow – had fans alright... but as their influence grew, the authorities were quick to realize the power a packed terrace could hold and acted to shut them down. Organized support and 'performance' were banned – as was travelling to away games.

These weren't hooligans getting arrested; these boys weren't being hauled off and banged up for rioting, assault or public order offences... they were marked men simply for following a football team. Just being a football fan, standing up and declaring your allegiance to your club, was enough to get you nicked.

It wasn't until Gorbachev came into power and instigated Perestroika and the move towards capitalism, that things began to change. Not just for football fans – for every part of Russian society. In the decade and a half since the Iron Curtain came down, the place has made up for lost time.

There are eight million people in Moscow now – and more billionaires than any other city in Europe. But not everyone has benefited from the country's embracing of the new order. There has been a flipside. For every businessman with big grins and billions in the bank, there are thousands living on the breadline – or well below the breadline.

As we tramped through the freezing evening to meet one of Moscow's original terrace legends, we cut straight through the contrasts. We passed waif-thin old ladies begging for pennies under neon Coca Cola signs, sick-looking prostitutes shivering outside McDonald's, hollow-eyed kids in alleys under the shadow of casinos, watching tourists and foreign businessmen in suits that cost more than they'd ever make in their lives... even a bunch of ignorant lumps like us could see what was happening. Democracy has brought an unprecedented freedom to Russia – but it's come at a price. The rich are becoming super rich – and the poor are getting flushed away.

Russia, it seems, doesn't do compromise. It's a country of extremes. It's either full-on communism... or rampant out-of-control capitalism. And whichever way it's gone, it's usually the ordinary people who come out worst.

Sergei Mitjakov – 'Every man is looking for a way to freedom. I have always thought football gave us that possibility.'

Before we could start to get our head round the current scene in Russia, we had to understand just what it was like being a football fan here before capitalism.

In the 1970s and 80s, as the rest of the world embraced the English Disease and hooliganism spread like wildfire across terraces from East London to Argentina, Russia stood alone. They didn't suffer from the riots and pitch invasions here – because Russian fans were not even allowed to clap for their teams.

There were pockets of rebellion, however. And one man more than any other helped bring about change on the terraces. Sergei Mitjakov is a Spartak Moscow legend – he's the man who almost single-handedly created Russian football support.

We met him in his tiny flat in a block in one of Moscow's shabbier districts. These estates have not felt the Midas touch of the new world order just yet – still blank and grey and peeling at the edges, they look now pretty much exactly as they would have looked 25 years ago.

Until you open the door to Sergei's flat. Inside it's a riot of red and white: posters, pennants, shields and banners cover the walls and all of them testament to his extreme love of his team. It's like a shrine to Spartak; like a temple to the club. (And given what he's gone through for them, you can't help feeling they should be building a shrine to him.)

'I have a humble home,' he said, as we all squeezed in. 'But I am rich in my heart.'

Now 50, he's a shortish, genial looking man. He made us all a cup of something hot he claimed was tea but had a serious kick to it, sat us in his kitchen, and told us how he got hooked. He was seven when he attended his first game – and it changed his life.

THE REAL FOOTBALL FACTORIES

'Second of May 1963,' he said, '103,000 people in the Lushenko stadium, no individual seats, the stadium was packed, people in the walkways... my father took me to the game and I was deliriously happy. Spartak beat CSKA Moscow 3-0, and after the football the grown-ups carried me to the metro station, they gave me chocolates and sweets, I was happy beyond measure.' There were tears in his eyes. 'That day I remember all my life,' he said, and swallowed hard.

Stan raised his eyebrows at Danny.

'So, um, you started going whenever you could, yeah?' said Peter quickly. 'And, it's hard to imagine for us, when you were a kid, in the stadium, no one clapped or cheered, everyone was silent?'

'Yeah, silence,' he said. 'You were not allowed to clap, by order of the militia. The party bosses said "Why do they hail Spartak? Why don't they hail the Party?" Informal public assemblies weren't welcomed at that time, we had a one party system, there was only the Communist Party. So they gave the order to the militia: we were not allowed to clap or cheer anything but the Party. And if we did we would be arrested.'

Nevertheless, despite the lack of atmosphere, Spartak became Sergei's life. He gathered together a small gang of similarly enthusiastic fans and together they set about building a whole Russian terrace culture – from scratch.

'When we created this group of Spartak fanatics, it was 20 or 30 people to start with,' he explained. 'We got together, we thought of chants and clapping, we invented all sorts of chants, rhymes and verses, we composed songs...

'There were no scarves, shirts, sweaters or hats then, we did that ourselves. Our mothers and grandmothers knitted them for us, we made our own flags and we went to the

169

stadium with these things and every time the police took them off us. We tried to express ourselves and we were constantly forbidden to do so. We had a constant struggle with the authorities.'

Eventually, the authorities became so concerned about the threat of Sergei's prototype firm that they cracked down on them – even though their worst crimes had been to wear scarves and sing the odd song.

'Our group grew and the powers obviously didn't like that,' he said. 'The militia terrorized us, they collected us and put us in prison many times. We were put there for one day, a few days, even for 15 days one time... and each time the offence was the same: "Organizer of disorder in the stadium".'

'What was the disorder?' asked Stan.

'We shouted 'Spartak forward!', 'Spartak Champion!' And we clapped a bit. It was seen as a violation of the communist regime.'

Still, Sergei's small firm grew – and in June 1977 even organized what is recognized as the first ever Russian away day. Forty-four of them hired a bus and made the long journey to Minsk, capital of Belarus. As travelling to away matches was banned at the time, they had to make up a suitable cover story.

'We told the tour agency we were going to a wedding,' he laughed, raising his cup of tea as Stan and Danny started laughing along. 'We pretended one of us was a groom and everything, we saved all our money, hired a bus for two days and just went. That was the first football away trip in the Soviet Union.'

He started dabbing at his eyes again. 'After the match in Minsk, Nicolai Petrovich Starostin, the patriarch of Spartak, the founder of Spartak, a man who was and is adored by the whole football community, he came to me at the bus and shook my hand and said "Young man, you have done a great deed". I didn't wash this hand for a week.'

Sergei and his tiny crew were not just football fans – they were part of the counter revolution. They helped to sow the seeds of rebellion, they helped to challenge Soviet control, and, ultimately, they helped overthrow the communist dictatorship. And they did it by going to football matches.

'Every man is looking for a way to freedom,' he said, as he showed us out of his simple flat and back into the icy Moscow night. 'I have always thought football gave us that possibility.'

Russian football fans today enjoy unprecedented freedoms. And for increasing numbers of them, the freedom that men like Sergei struggled so hard to win for them manifests itself in one simple way: by kicking the shit out of each other every weekend.

'I hope they're grateful,' muttered Stan.

If Sergei represented the birth of Spartak support, we wanted to see how it is on the terraces now. We were on the trail of the new enemies of the state.

•   •   •

Spartak Moscow is the most successful club in Russian history, with more than 20 league championships to their name. They're also just about the most glamorous too – and thanks to the sudden boom in Russian wealth, are set to benefit from a new state-of-the-art £80 million stadium. Considering the average annual wage here is around £4,000, that's a mad sum of money – and proportionally at least, puts even the likes of Chelsea in the shade.

But if they have been among the first to benefit from the new regime here, Spartak were also right at the forefront of Russian hooliganism.

It took half a decade after the collapse of communism – but when it did happen, there was no mistaking it.

Eight days at the end of summer 1997 established the way it was going to be. First, on 23 August, as Spartak and deadly local rivals CSKA Moscow met on the pitch, 300 of their fans clashed in a park in the city. The police were totally unprepared – they had never seen anything like it before – and dozens were seriously injured before anything like order was restored.

When the wounded were counted, it was generally acknowledged that CSKA won the day... which is why a week later the Spartak firms set about recapturing some lost pride. Two hundred of them ambushed a huge group of Zenit St Petersburg fans as they made their way through the city. Despite being outnumbered more than two to one, the Spartak lads smashed their way through the Zenit ranks – over 150 were arrested and many of the St Petersburg firm were hospitalized.

A pattern was set – and throughout the following seasons Spartak firms were involved in clashes more or less every week, often inside the stadiums themselves. Inspired by the English crews of the 1980s, they even modelled themselves in the Casuals style. Suddenly Umbro, Lonsdale, Lacoste all became big names in Russian fashion – by the turn of the millennium, a typical weekend on the terraces would see ranks of the Spartak hardcore looking as sharp as the Liverpool kop circa 1984.

The style has stuck. And it was going to be our way into one of Spartak's oldest and most vicious mobs.

The Gladiators of Spartak Moscow – 'Win or die'
Spartak might have been the oldest and most distinctive mobbed-up team in Russia – but access to the men that matter in their firms was not easy. Perhaps because they're the team that everyone else in the country hates, perhaps because all those years of communist repression has left them naturally suspicious, or perhaps because they didn't think much of us personally, they were being a little bit evasive.

But Peter was adamant. We couldn't come to Russia and not hear the modern voice of Spartak hooliganism. Sergei had given us history and tradition – we needed to hear what it was like now.

After two days of negotiations and blind alleys, finally, one of our local contacts came through. He had been in touch with a man who ran a clothes shop downtown... and who could also be found at every home game leading the chants on the Spartak terraces.

His name was Ivan Katanaev – and he was practically the outfitter to Spartak's nastiest supporters. He agreed to meet us... and if he liked us well enough, he would introduce us to the top boy of the Gladiators.

'Don't fuck this up,' said Peter, as we left the hotel, stepping out into the black and neon Moscow night wrapped up in parkas and woolly hats pulled down low.

Stan nodded at Danny. 'Yeah, this is serious Dan,' he said. 'Don't fuck it up.'

Peter shook his head. 'I wasn't talking to him,' he said. 'Danny – you do your thing. Stan – just, um, don't do yours...'

Inside Ivan's shop, Danny eased into charm mode, every inch the approachable movie star, the geezer next door from the telly, the man who could probably sort you out with the model's mobile number and the VIP pass...

'You got some great clobber here,' he said, shaking Ivan's hand and casting an appreciative eye around the rails. 'Stone Island, Hackett, Lambretta, Henri Lloyd...' He picked up a coat. 'I might buy this. This is a sweet bit of gear. What do you want for this?'

Ivan grinned. He was sold.

The next night saw us at Ivan's clothes shop again (Danny did buy the coat in the end: at £300 it was the equivalent of about a month's wage for the average football fan here) and after he locked up, we followed him further into town. He led us away from the McDonalds and the casinos and the bustling crowds of sightseers and into the back room of a bar off an alley at the end of a street where the tourists don't go.

Inside, three men sat at a table. Two of them were your typical big lugs – and exactly what we'd expect from Russian football yobs: all muscles and wife-beater vests, baseball caps low over long hair, tattoos, stubble – but the man in the middle was like no other hooligan we'd met.

He was dressed all in black – black trainers, tight black jeans, tight black polo neck sweater and black balaclava. He sat with his hands fixed on the table in front of him, eyes downcast like he was meditating.

He looked like a ninja. His name was Vasilli The Killer. His firm were one of Spartak's oldest and most vicious: named in honour of Spartacus himself, they took the Gladiators' slogan for their own. Every member had a tattoo on his right breast with the ancient Roman motto: win or die.

He motioned to an empty seat opposite. Danny sat down – everyone else stood behind. Slowly he raised his eyes and stared at each of us in turn. Stan's smile froze on his lips.

'Ask me anything,' Vasilli said, still fixing Stan with furious eyes.

'Why do they call you the Killer?' whispered Stan.

One of Vasilli's henchmen leaned forward and addressed his answer to Danny. 'They call him that because he never takes any prisoners,' he said, slowly.

'Okay,' nodded Danny, offering cigarettes around, 'that's cool. The Killer. Cool. Like it. Snappy. Nice one... so how did you get involved with all this then, Killer?'

Vasilli turned his stare to Danny. 'I became a hooligan 12 years ago,' he said, 'when The Gladiators first started. And I did it because I don't want to be an average man, I don't want to be like everybody else.

'I think at the beginning, the whole Russian hooliganism went the English way, in my view, not the entirely right way. But with the years, we took some good and bad things they knew, stuff from Poland, England, Italy, and so on. I think at the end of the day Russian football hooliganism found its own way.'

Danny asked him what their own way entailed.

'The way we fight in Russia: they don't fight like that in Europe. We only use knuckles, fists. Nobody uses weapons like they do over there. This is the main difference – that's why if you want to win in a fight, you need to be very strong.'

He leaned forward over the table and fixed Danny straight in the eye.

'If you want to be a member of The Gladiators, you need to be a sportsman, you need to go to the gym, to go boxing. All of our top boys, all our top hooligans, they go to the gym, they train themselves.

'Unlike in Europe, in Russia things happen all year round; it doesn't even have to be a matchday. I can come out of a pub and a group of guys attack me and I'll fight them – that can happen any time. A fight can happen any day, it's a proper war that goes on.'

'And what's in it for you?' asked Danny. 'What do you get out of fighting for Spartak?'

He thought for a second. 'For me, a fight is like adrenaline poisoning the bloodstream,' he said, 'and at the peak of the adrenaline rush, you have to seize it... if you seize it, then it helps you in the fight, it heightens your reaction and strength. If you don't seize it and it poisons you, then the fight is lost. It's an amazing feeling.

'I've seen everything that can happen. I've seen one of our Gladiator brothers seriously injured by a Dinamo supporter – he was in a coma for more than two weeks, he's just learning to talk and walk again. These things happen. We all know what we're in for; it's everyone's own choice, a choice everyone makes.'

He hadn't blinked once the whole time we had been there and by now he was staring full on at Danny, inches away from his face. Stan and Peter were close to freaking out, but Danny was keeping it together.

'So I'm thinking, what you really want to do is fight the English?' he asked. 'Are the English like... an ambition for you?'

Peter was about to call time on the interview, but Vasilli was talking and Stan kept the camera rolling.

'I personally spit on the English,' he said. 'I think the British scene ended already at the end of the 80s, when the police started to contain them; and now they don't dare to do a thing, right now they're all fat, sitting in the pub and drinking Guinness, content to throw a few chairs around at the World Cup. They're rubbish, drugs addicts and alcoholics. I don't see any strength there at all.'

'So you do want to take them on then?' said Danny.

'I'll answer very short and clear,' he replied. 'Everything will happen. Expect us. The door is open: we will soon step through it.'

He stood up. 'That's it,' he announced, turned around, and walked away.

We looked at each other. Danny slumped in his seat.

'We're leaving. Right now,' said Peter.

• • •

If Vasilli and his Gladiators were intimidating enough in their contempt for the English, it was nothing compared to how they feel about their cross-town rivals CSKA Moscow.

Their hatred for each other is the equal to anything the world over – and it's been made worse by the change in fortunes of the clubs. Where Spartak has traditionally been the dominant side, since the turn of the millennium CSKA have caught up. They won the Russian Championship three times in the four years from 2003, twice doing the double with the Russian Cup – and in 2005 became the first Russian side to lift a major European trophy when they beat Sporting Lisbon in Portugal to win the UEFA Cup.

Watching their enemy winning has been hard for the likes of The Gladiators. And as the teams have fought for supremacy, so have their firms.

The 2001 derby game was typical. For days before the fixture rumours had been buzzing around the city as to where the firms were going to clash. Appeals for calm were made in the run up to the game – they were ignored. Finally, on matchday morning, flashpoints of trouble flared up around the city – 80 Spartak fans ambushed a small group of CSKA hooligans near the train station, another group clashed in a park on the other side of town – but these were just dummy runs, diversions, warm-ups to the main event.

Hours before kick off a huge brawl erupted in the city centre: official reports have it that 500 hooligans armed with knives, iron bars, broken bottles and baseball bats laid into each other and, as the police struggled to contain them, they were joined by greater numbers – the fights continuing all the way down to the stadium and on to the terraces.

Although both sides claimed not to have used weapons, there were hundreds injured – some with the kind of slash wounds and broken bones you simply can't get from bare knuckles. Whatever: the end result was over 300 arrests and the day going the way of The Gladiators.

The night CSKA raised the UEFA Cup in 2005 saw another victory for the Spartak firms. A mob of 70 or so hooligans charged a CSKA pub at 1am as celebrations were in full swing. Within minutes the pub was trashed; by the time the police got there the only bodies left were two fans bleeding on the floor.

CSKA swore revenge – and within a year the roles were reversed. And next on our agenda was a meeting with a man who was there when the firms from CSKA claimed dominance in this town.

THE REAL FOOTBALL FACTORIES

The Gallant Steeds of CSKA Moscow – 'The important thing is: you have to overcome your fear'

CSKA stands for Central Sporting Club of the Army: they were founded by the Soviet military and during the communist era had a reputation as being the State's 'favoured' team. Their nickname of 'the horses' comes from this time – it was said that the CSKA coaches picked the best players from the conscript ranks like they were picking horses.

It's perhaps fitting then, that in the bright new capitalist Russia, the sporting figurehead of the old regime has recently benefitted from a massive cash injection thanks to a sponsorship deal with an oil company connected with one of the country's new billionaires.

Times are good for this club. And if the boys from Spartak were being all cloak and dagger with us, the lads from CSKA's brightest, boldest, most fearless up-and-coming firm were only too happy to meet us.

They had to be a little bit careful, of course. We were told to get in our hire car and start driving… we'd get a call confirming the venue when they were sure we weren't being followed.

When that call came, it took us all by surprise. We were directed to the club's headquarters itself – a massive concrete complex built for the Red Army that's now home to the CSKA hockey, athletics and football clubs. Inside, we were told, bold as brass, were waiting some lads from the Gallant Steeds – a young mob making a big name for themselves.

'You've got to love their cheek,' said Stan, peering out of the window at the drizzle and the slush as we pulled into the car park and were met by a man in zipped up anorak and sunglasses. 'Can you imagine the Headhunters meeting a TV crew in Chelsea Village? Fucking cheeky bastards!'

Our boy in the anorak and shades led us through massive iron gates and down stairs into a huge bar, where he introduced Cashpoint, top boy of Gallant Steeds.

Where Vasilli and The Gladiators had been intimidating, Cashpoint was totally charming. 'Hi, hi, pleased to meet you,' he said, indicating where he'd already got us litre jugs of beer each. He was dressed in jeans and a cream jumper and looked a bit like David Walliams. 'Shall we go through to where it's quieter?' he said and, as we all picked up our beers, he offered to meet us again the next day for a quick tour of his firm's greatest battlefields before getting us into the CSKA v Zenit St Petersburg game.

'First of all,' he said, 'I'd like to thank the British for introducing football hooliganism to us; thank you for the idea.'

Stan laughed. 'No worries,' he said. 'Um – a pleasure I guess.'

'It's really a pity that these banning orders, these CCTV cameras, made you stop your activities, made you stop being the number one in the world,' he continued, shaking his head. 'But still – full respect from our side and please, don't be afraid to fight Russians when you get the chance.'

We were liking Cashpoint already.

'For me personally,' he said, 'this has been a big part of my life. I'm running with the firm since I was 15, and it gave me a chance to expand my mind, to open my mind for a different view in life. I used to be the smallest one and all the boys told me "you go boxing"... and now?' he flexed his muscles and we could see that under his jumper he was powerfully built. 'Now I'm thinking of boxing professionally.'

The Gallant Steeds are relative newcomers to the Moscow scene, but built up a reputation fast through the simple tactic of ambushing rival firms as they travelled to games on the trains.

'We had spotters on a couple of platforms,' he explained. 'So we're standing, ready, mob-handed waiting for them. When the train comes we already knew what cars they were in... we'd pull the emergency break so they couldn't get away and then we would smash into them.' He grinned. 'We were building our name on these trains, smashing the mobs coming into Moscow from the suburbs. It gave us a really hard reputation.'

Peter took the chance to ask him about something that had been on our minds, something that Vasilli had mentioned. 'Tell us about how you fight,' he said, 'is it just bare knuckles or are there weapons?'

'There is a code of honour,' he nodded. 'Sometimes people use weapons, but inside the firm we have a strict rule, a code, and if someone tries to use a bottle or a knife or something else in a fight, he gets thrown out.

'It's a part of Russian tradition, there has been bare knuckle fighting throughout the history of Russia. We're following those principles of the fair fight. If you don't follow them you should be ashamed, you will be branded a coward.'

We were all gobsmacked. We were used to an anything-goes mentality among hoolies, an all's-fair-in-hate-and-war attitude. We'd been to places where the boys carried guns, machetes, bombs even. How could they hope to compete against that?

'We have training sessions,' said Cashpoint. 'We train not just one on one, but all together – so we divide our mob into equal parts and fight each other. We're coming from a sporting style of life and going for martial arts, boxing, karate, judo.'

He smiled. 'Anything can happen to you, when you're

doing this football violence. Sometimes you win and sometimes you lose. The important thing is: you have to overcome your fear.'

If that was a surprise, Cashpoint had a bigger one up his sleeve. One of his boys introduced Svetlana, a blonde, willowy girl in her mid-twenties with a shy smile and a low-cut top.

Stan and Peter looked at each other. 'Corporate hospitality,' whispered Stan, with a wink.

He couldn't have been more wrong. Svetlana was top girl in CSKA's first female firm. The pretty face and smiling eyes hid a hooligan's heart.

Danny laughed. 'You're joking?' he said. 'She looks so innocent!'

'She's a kickboxer,' warned Cashpoint, 'be careful of her, man.'

It seemed that Svetlana's little mob formed after feeling frustrated at not getting a part of the boys' action on the terraces. There have always been women in the Russian Army – why not in the firms too? CSKA is, after all, the army team.

She spoke and Cashpoint translated for us. 'She says they are trying to show that they're not just women who go to the football, but that she's determined to defend her colours at the same level as guys. So they fight the same as the guys fight, no biting or pulling hair or scratching – just like we might fight. Exactly the same. Except that many of the girls also do kickboxing, of course.'

Danny asked what they got out of it in terms of adrenaline.

She talked for a while and Cashpoint frowned. 'That's probably hard to describe,' he said, 'every person gets a different rush. She says it's like how some people go parachuting and get pleasure from that, others go up steep mountains and get pleasure from that... and she gets her rush from fighting. It's a different rush, but it's the same in the sense that it's also an extreme sport.'

'I can't get over this,' said Danny, 'she looks so sweet! How could anyone hit that face?'

She smiled at him. 'Have you got a message for English female fans darlin'?' he asked.

She didn't need Cashpoint for that one. 'Watch out!' she said. 'We're coming for your women!'

• • •

The next day we hooked up with Cashpoint again – this time at his gym. He wasn't joking about his professional prospects – the boy's a useful boxer and looks like he could take it as well as dish it out. Peter wanted to film him training and, as we watched him bob and weave around the ring, we began to see the value in this strange Code of Honour the Russian hooligans subscribed to.

'Question,' said Stan. 'So you've got a bottle and Cashpoint here's just got his fists. Would you take him on?'

We watched him lay a quick one-two-one into the punchbag. We felt the impact even from 10 feet away, the whump-thump-chump. Dust and sweat flew. Stan winced.

'Actually,' he continued, answering his own question, 'Forget it. No fucking chance. Not if there were six of us with samurai swords.'

Cashpoint had got us tickets for the match, but first he wanted to take us to the site of his firm's greatest victory – and the place that in 2006 saw CSKA claim supremacy over all Moscow.

1905 Street is a bit like Leicester Square – surrounded by shops, cinemas, all the bright hustle and bustle of a capital city centre. A tube station stands at one end – a massive multi-storey McDonald's at another. But at 3pm on a Saturday afternoon in 2006, the shoppers and tourists were left running for their lives as the big firms from Spartak and CSKA came together for their most defining battle yet.

Cashpoint stood under a huge statue commemorating the revolutionary uprising. Around us taxis and trams and people all hurried by. It was hard to imagine the scenes he was describing:

'So our mob was standing there,' he said, pointing to one end of the square, 'there were about 200 of us... and then the Spartak firm appeared, they came out of the tube station. We stood facing each other, lining up like armies in our battle rows...'

The stand-off was short-lived, a second or two of calm before the storm. Even as shoppers, tourists and passers-by began to realize what was about to happen and ran to get out of the way, the two mobs charged each other.

'We met right in the middle of the road,' he said, 'so the traffic was blocked and our mobs clashed right in the middle, we were pushing them and beating them back. There were about 400 people fighting, them and us together, about equal numbers on each side.'

The CSKA and Spartak firms tore into each other, toe-to-toe, fist-to-fist, fighting hand-to-hand like two ancient armies. No quarter was given or taken – the pride and fury of the whole city was felt by both sides.

Men and boys dropped and lay where they fell, stepped over or trampled as the fight raged around them: the square was stained with their blood. And in the end the tide slowly but irresistibly turned the way of the Gallant Steeds. 'We were all marching down the road, so we absolutely blocked the traffic on that day. It was a great reason to celebrate, it was a really great victory over them,' he said, clapping his hands and staring up at the statue. 'Half of them ran and half of them were lying unconscious; that's why we won.'

Danny asked about civilian casualties, innocent passers-by, shoppers, tourists – what did they make of 400 hooligans tearing up around them?

Cashpoint slapped him on the back. 'They enjoyed the view! It's not every day that you can see 400 men clashing right on the road near the tube station... so a lot of them got their mobile phones and started filming, so now we can watch it again on the internet. So that was really a nice thing, I think, yes?'

Everyone laughed – and promised Cashpoint that we would be sure to look him up on Youtube when we got home, as well as tell everyone we knew about the fearless fighters of CSKA Moscow.

We didn't think it was a good idea to tell Cashpoint that just a few days before we'd been sat in a pub with the top boy of his sworn enemies, The Gladiators of Spartak Moscow... but as it turned out we didn't need to. Word about our activities was already on the street. And some of the CSKA boys weren't exactly happy about it.

CSKA v Zenit St Petersburg – 'You better leave now – while you still can'

The atmosphere outside the Dinamo Stadium was eerie. On the one hand there were all the usual trappings of a top-of-a-table clash – the gangs of lads laughing, chanting, pushing and shoving, the little kids in matching hat-and-scarf sets, holding hands with their dads, the stalls selling tat, the vans dishing out hot drinks and rank burgers… and then there were the long, thick, bristling ranks of the armed forces: helmets, combat fatigues, guns and dogs, truncheons and shields.

But most of all it was cold. Colder than anything any of us had ever known. It was minus four before you counted the wind chill factor – and it was not the weather for standing on a football terrace.

'I can see the appeal of being a hooligan here,' said Stan, 'at least it keeps you warm, you know what I mean?'

The strangest thing of all, however, was the reaction of the other CSKA fans. Cashpoint told us to stick close – but it seemed that to these Muscovites Danny was a hero.

We were used to his being recognized a bit… we didn't realize just how huge *The Football Factory* was over here. It was proper celebrity time; Danny was mobbed. He spent an hour out there in the freezing cold before kick off just signing autographs, his numb fingers scribbling on tickets, fag packets, even people's arms.

'They love you,' laughed Cashpoint.

Before the game was over those same boys would be looking at us with different eyes altogether.

The match itself passed without incident. We were hemmed in one end; the 5,000 traveling fans from St Petersburg pinned in the other. Below us, stone-faced soldiers in thick hats and combat gear stared at us throughout.

The cold seemed to bleed through into the very way the Russians support their teams. There were none of the flags, banners, dancing or exuberance of the Mediterranean or

South American sides... rather there were low, guttural chants, deep rolling songs, and a weird thing where everyone linked arms and stamped their feet.

It was half-time when Peter began to get nervous. He nudged Stan; he'd become aware of whispers, low conversations, people pointing at us. The previously friendly faces and big grins had been replaced by frowns, sneers, what sounded more like insults.

'What's the score, Cashpoint?' asked Danny. 'Are we cool?'

Cashpoint had been in heated conversation with some fans who had made their way up towards us. He waved them away and turned to us.

It seemed that word had got around about our meeting with Vasilli and The Gladiators of Spartak. The rank-and-file CSKA fans weren't happy about our hobnobbing with their most hated enemies; there were rumbles of discontent, whispers that we should be taught a lesson, made an example of.

'I think you're safe with me,' said Cashpoint, 'but if my back turns for a minute... who knows? Perhaps you better leave now. While you still can.'

We waited for the second half to get going and then slipped out. Cashpoint was a good geezer and we didn't want to take the piss – and, as Stan pointed out, we really didn't want to be made an example of either.

If Moscow was no longer so safe for us, we were headed north. We were going to follow the Zenit fans all the way back to St Petersburg. And while we were there, we were going to find the future of Russian football hooliganism.

• • •

It was snowing in St Petersburg.

'Minus four in Moscow and what do we do?' grumbled Stan. 'We head 400 miles north. Brilliant.'

St Petersburg is the former capital of Russia and is a city soaked in history. Peter – a man who knows about such things – told us that it's been seen as Russia's centre of culture and great thinkers since it was founded... and also known as a place of incredible suffering, enormous sacrifice. It was the home of the novelist Dostoyevsky and the composer Shostakovich – as well as the Russian Tsars who ruled before the 1917 Revolution... and the peasants who deposed them.

There are fantastic palaces, beautiful buildings, incredible monuments in this city... but also vast no-go areas, crumbling tenement blocks, collapsing estates, and a history of violence and bloodshed more brutal than anywhere else in Russia.

It was here that the Revolution began – millions of the poor rose up and stormed the palaces, overthrowing their leaders and tearing up the status quo in favour of new ideals. St Petersburg became Leningrad, Stalin took power and for many the beautiful revolutionary ideals became a sordid mess, a struggle just to survive.

Start to look into St Petersburg's bloody past and the numbers get silly. After the Revolution, it's reckoned some nine million people died in five years of civil war and famine – and after Stalin took power he's thought to have overseen the deaths of anything up to 35 million more supposed 'enemies of the state'. Between 1917 and 1930 two million people 'disappeared' from St Petersburg alone; and during the Second World War, when the Germans laid siege to the city for 29 months, over one million people died from starvation and disease – nearly half the city's population at the time.

And still – they didn't give in. They kept going, kept fighting. They're used to hardship here. They're used to fighting through the pain.

And now, with the country undergoing another revolution, we were here because we'd heard that the boys from Zenit St Petersburg had designs on re-establishing their city as Russia's number one.

Zenit are a team on the up, a club looking to challenge Moscow's dominance. With some big-money backers behind them they've been putting the performances in on the pitch and are set to benefit from a brand new multi-million pound stadium. And off the pitch they're a rising force too.

We'd come here to meet what some are calling the future of Russian hooliganism – the first Superfirm.

Music Hall of Zenit St Petersburg – 'There's no better feeling than when you walk out, mobbed up with your mates... you see your enemies, blood shoots to your head...'
We had been set up with Alexander, a bright, polite, well-groomed 23-year-old who also happens to be one of the founders of the only firm outside the capital that commands universal respect in Russia. Music Hall have only been around since 2004 and they were formed as a kind of alliance of all the best of the other Zenit firms.

'They're like a crack unit,' explained Peter as we were taken into a pub opposite the stadium; and as we peeled off layers of scarves, hats, coats and jumpers, Alexander sat in an open-necked shirt and jeans, face mostly hidden behind huge sunglasses and a friendly smile on his face. He raised a hand at someone behind us and litre jugs of beers appeared.

'Cheers!' said Danny, blowing on his hands and offering cigarettes around. 'I could do with something to warm me up...'

Stan sorted out vodka chasers while Alexander explained the thinking behind Music Hall.

'When we started our firm,' he said simply, 'it was formed out of the best. In 2004 on the 31st of July, it was created from the best fighters of all the different Zenit firms.'

Danny asked where the strange name came from. 'Music Hall,' he said, 'no offence or anything, but it's not exactly that intimidating is it?'

Alexander smiled. 'Everyone has these scary names – "gladiators", things like that... and we thought: we're cheerful fellas and we like to fight. We thought of calling ourselves "Pamela Anderson" at first, just as a joke, then we named ourselves "Music Hall" because we go into a fight with a smile, because for us it's comical, it's fun, it's not tragic.'

'You so should have stuck with Pamela Anderson,' laughed Stan. 'Fucking priceless. "Run! It's Pamela Anderson!"; "Pamela Anderson's after us!"; "I got fucked by Pamela Anderson!" Brilliant.'

'It's a good joke,' agreed Alexander. 'We even wanted to make a T-shirt for ourselves "Pamela Anderson loves Music Hall".'

There's not too much in the way of smiles when this firm get to business, however. In their first three years they'd taken on the big Moscow players in a series of carefully staged – and flawlessly executed – battles. With no real opposition locally, they've mostly saved themselves for the capital's big two: and, at first at least, they caught them napping. Their reputation was sealed after a massive confrontation with Spartak – hundreds on both sides came together wielding nothing but fists... but still so ferociously that it took riot police with truncheons and dogs hours to get the battle fully under control.

Almost everybody came away from that one with some kind of scar – most of the combatants were hospitalized.

It was weird: Alexander was clearly a smart boy, intelligent, savvy, funny – what was he doing running with a hooligan firm, let alone leading one?

'Oh, we've got many different types in our crew,' he explained, 'we've got lawyers and business men, we've got sailors, there's sportsmen, there's shop workers and shop owners, all kinds. But when we go on the street and meet our opponents, all the differences disappear. We don't care about who is who in their normal lives, there's no hierarchy, there's just move forward and get the enemy down.

'You could say we're a family. Even though we've only been a firm for a couple of years I know most of the people already for 10 years. Everyone is my brother and I can answer for all of them.'

'So why do you do it?' asked Danny.

He leaned forward and grinned. 'There's no better feeling than when you walk out, mobbed up with your mates, you feel their strength, you feel your brothers next to you, you walk shoulder to shoulder, you see your enemies, blood shoots to your head...

'The fight itself is no big deal, the fight itself is just work, you just do your thing – but when you feel the strength of your mates and you feel the strength of the enemies, it's a mind blowing feeling. It's better than an orgasm, you have to try it once, and once you have, it's hard to stop, it's a drug. If you like it, you'll be a hooligan for life.'

If Alexander and Music Hall are representative of Russia's new hooligan order, they're also fierce believers in the 'Fair Play' we'd heard about: organized fights of equal numbers, without weapons, pre-arranged and conducted without any innocent civilian casualties.

'In St Petersburg we only do Fair Play,' he said. 'Fighters show their strength only when they fight with their knuckles. Using weapons… that's not about strength. Anyone can use a knife, anyone can fire a gun.

'And we're all Russians, we don't want to kill each other. This – I love it, but it's nothing but a hobby. It's our hobby, and to use it to kill your fellow countrymen and comrades, that's awful. Killing is not good. But we fight, and they break my nose, that's funny, that's okay, in the morning the pain is gone. You laugh about it, you think to yourself: that was a good fight yesterday, tomorrow I will break their noses…

'At the end of the day, we don't see anything criminal in what we do, we just fight with people who also want to fight. We don't start a fight on the street with some passer-by, we don't start fights in clubs or bars. I don't need that, I'm happy with my football fights. So I hope that the police don't see anything wrong with what we do – we don't report anything, why should anyone report us?'

It was beautifully logical. The way Alexander talked about it, the firms weren't criminals, outlaws to be hunted down and banned and thrown in jail – they were simply practising a sort of extreme sport. They were all consenting adults, they all knew what they were doing – and by adhering to a code of honour and an organizational structure that kept numbers even and weapons banned, they were making sure that clashes between firms were, like sport itself, tests of strength, endurance and skill... and not numbers, or who's the most tooled up.

'Would it work in England?' wondered Danny out loud.

'Would it fuck,' said Stan. 'Someone's always going to raise the stakes, someone's always going to go too far. There's too many psychos. People in England don't become hoolies to follow rules, do they?'

It also struck us that there's something else going on here as well. Everything we had seen of Russia seemed to suggest that it was a country barely containing the wild excesses of its new capitalist ideology. The whole place was losing its identity in a whirl of consumerism and corporate cash – big money was making big changes and the little guys were getting forgotten about or trampled on in the process.

These boys, however, were fighting back. They were imposing order, structure, discipline on their own lives. They were taking control. They were doing it the only way they knew how... they were doing it in a totally Russian way – through nothing but the power of their own fists.

'Our mentality is probably different from the English one,' shrugged Alexander, 'we have harder fights I guess. In Russia from childhood onwards there are fights everyday after school, there's always fights on the streets... maybe that's why we've got this kind of hooliganism.'

He grinned and raised his glass. 'Although of course, I very much respect English fighters,' he said. 'I would love to have a fight with you sometime.'

CHAPTER EIGHT

TURKEY

We know about Turkey, right? We know too much. When English fans come to Turkey it can prove fatal.

But we couldn't stay away. The Turkish firms are redefining the way football teams are supported. They're going beyond fanaticism, into something more vibrant – and more violent. We had to taste it for ourselves… and that meant getting down there, down where the adrenaline's flowing hardest.

Istanbul, the capital, is a city of clashing continents, cultures and football clubs. This is where old meets new, East meets West, and, increasingly often, where football equals fatalities. We'd come to a society we couldn't hope to fully understand, to sample a code of living based on honour, revenge and the blade.

People are prepared to kill for their team here.

We were way out of our depth.

Welcome to Hell.

There's no point in pretending otherwise. Two names were on our minds in the run-up to arriving in Turkey. Those two names would stay with us throughout our time here. And, truth be told, they had been lurking in the back of our minds ever since we first knew we'd be coming to Istanbul.

Christopher Loftus and Kevin Speight were both killed in this city; knifed to death for the simple fact that they were Leeds United fans. They were not part of any firm, they weren't even hooligans: they were just unlucky enough to be caught in the wrong place at the wrong time. You could say they were unlucky that other English fans had wound up the locals that night; that they were unlucky that the Galatasaray fans reacted in such an extreme manner; or that the police were so slow to react; or even that they were unlucky that Leeds had drawn Galatasaray in the UEFA Cup at all.

Or you could say they were inevitable victims of Turkey's volatile mix of football fanaticism, knife culture and fervent honour code. You could say that if it wasn't them it would have been someone else.

Doesn't change the fact they're dead though.

Christopher Loftus and Kevin Speight. Whatever else happened in Turkey, whatever else we would see and whoever else we would meet, have a laugh with, share a drink with... or try to stay away from – it was their names that were always with us. An awful lot has been said and written about those two boys – and even as we were there the whole thing hadn't been properly resolved – but as far as we could tell, the bottom line is pretty simple. They shouldn't have died. We tried not to forget it.

• • •

'Right,' said Danny, blowing out his cheeks. 'Turkey. What do we know? We're in Europe, right? But we're also in Asia? Or is that Asia over there?' he pointed across the Bosphorus, the great river splitting Istanbul in two. 'Either way they're in the Champions League, the Eurovision song contest. So if we're in Europe and also Asia then we got the Middle East sort of down the road there – Iraq and Iran just round the corner. Nice. Okay.

'What else? Bazaars, hubbly bubbly pipes and kebabs. Semi-finals of the World Cup 2002. Hakan Sukur. Muzzy Izzit. Fenerbahce and Galatasaray. Mental support. Proper mental. Dangerous. Pride and honour and revenge.

'What have I missed?'

'Knives,' said Peter.

We were all a bit nervous of Turkey – and not simply because of what happened between Galatasaray and Leeds back in April 2000. We were nervous because it seemed that, once you look into the football scene here, the idea of a couple of lads getting stabbed for supporting the wrong team isn't actually that unusual. We would come within minutes of seeing so for ourselves.

But nerves aside, we were going to treat this place the same as everywhere else we'd been.

We'd met the most vicious football fans in the world, we'd held our own with hooligans across three continents – and we'd always stayed professional. We treated everyone the same: we treated them all with respect. No matter what. And Turkey was going to have to be no different.

'Right,' said Danny again. 'When in Turkey, do as the Turkish do. You know how I like to experience different cultures. Let's get ourselves a nice cup of tea and one of those big fat bong things to suck on.'

The tea was bitter; the hookah pipes were huge. We all sucked hard.

'I'm getting nothing from this,' said Stan, sitting back with a sigh. 'Nothing at all.'

No matter how we were determined to play it, Turkey was different from everywhere else we'd been. Eighty per cent of the country lives below the poverty line, struggling between the ancient rural traditions and the influence of the bright, modern, throwaway world.

It's a country rushing to embrace all the immediacy and instant gratification of the 21st century West... while still holding on to philosophies handed down from generation-to-generation for as far back as anyone can remember. It doesn't always get the mix right.

Even its unique position on the map has made for a fierce history. Everyone from Alexander the Great onwards has fancied a piece of this place – and the capital city has had to keep changing its name to keep up with the troubles surrounding it: now Istanbul, it has been Constantinople and before that Byzantium.

All this strife in their past has made the Turkish people both very proud... and very hard. They're not used to taking things lying down. Honour and revenge are both ingrained in the national consciousness: insult them and they will strike back harder.

And that's not an idle boast. It can seem like everyone carries a knife in this town. As we would be told by a firm revelling in the name Kill For You: 'Knife culture is Turkish culture. It's not just football. Two guys can start fighting and it can be over anything and knives start talking.'

And now everyone's got football too.

THE REAL FOOTBALL FACTORIES

Istanbul is a city divided not only by the Bosphorus, by the jangling mix of ancient and modern, or even by the fact that half of it's in Asia and half in Europe... it's a city divided by football.

There are four teams here: Besiktas, Istanbulspor, Galatasaray and Fenerbahce... but the city is split by allegiance to the big two. Here, you're either a lion of Galatasaray or a canary of Fenerbahce. And you better be careful where and how loudly you shout about it, too. Galatasaray's Ali Sami Yen stadium is in the bustling, modern Taksim Square district in the European half of the city: Fener's Sukru Saracoglu stadium across the water in Asia.

Galatasaray were formed out of the elite high school, a club originally for the wealthy and privileged. Fenerbahce, on the other hand, have always been the people's team; and for their first few years existed as a kind of underground sports club, set apart from the official authorities.

And it was to the Asian half of the city we were headed. We were going to meet a man who would hopefully explain just what being a football fan means in this country.

'Somebody better wake up Stan,' said Peter, as we got up to leave.

Paul Okan of Fenerbahce – 'They were carrying these long knives, they were shooting each other, having wars in parks and fights outside the stadiums...'
It might have been the pipes we'd been smoking on, it might have been the jetlag catching up with us, it might even have been the tension... but things began to take a surreal twist. There were strange sights in the Sukru Saracoglu.

We were meeting Paul Okan outside Fenerbahce's ground.

The son of Turkish legend Ogun Altiparmak, who, much to Danny's excitement even got a game against Bobby Moore, he's well-known in Turkey for a documentary he made on the team's championship-winning 2005 season.

He wanted to take us round the ground as they were setting up ready for the next day's game – the big one, the derby, Fener versus Galatasaray... the game we had tickets for.

Paul was a friendly guy, short with long, slick, very black hair. He shook hands with us all, and immediately engaged Peter in conversation about camera equipment. He took us pitch-side and we watched as men scurried on the terraces with enormous flags.

'This is setting up?' asked Stan. 'Those guys – are they club officials or fans?'

Paul pointed out an older man strolling around the edge of the pitch. 'That's the club president,' he said. 'He likes to inspect the place. Sometimes I hear that he gets here in the middle of the night, like one in the morning, and he sits all by himself and smokes...'

Danny laughed: 'Like it... he's milking it for all its worth. Good on him.'

The rest of the figures scurrying across the terraces, however, were fans getting ready for tomorrow's match. Paul explained that the club allowed supporters' groups in early in order to arrange their banners properly for the big games – and also so they could run an eye over those banners themselves, check that the slogans on the flags were not overly offensive or likely to provoke the visiting fans into reacting too extremely.

'The clubs do not allow violence anymore in the stadiums,' he said. 'Well, not in this stadium anyway. You might catch it in away games or outside the stadium… but this stadium is clean, it's well screened.'

Danny whistled as a huge banner was unfurled: it covered most of one stand. 'Look at that,' he said. 'You would never get any of that back home. The fans would never be allowed in the stadiums in England… the way it is there is you pay your money and you fuck off.'

He pointed at a face on the flag and asked Paul if it was the founder of the club.

Paul looked grave. 'That is Kemal Ataturk,' he said. 'The founder of the Turkish republic.'

'Is he the one on the money?'

Paul nodded slowly.

'Thought I clocked that boat,' said Danny, brightly. Stan tried not to laugh.

Peter suggested we get on with it, and asked Paul what football meant to the average man in the street here.

'Football is more then a culture in Turkey,' he said. 'It is life itself, you know? Life in Turkey is pretty tough: people work hard and they do not make enough money. Some people have lots of money but most people are poor and they do not feel in control of their lives. But when they go to a stadium, it's like it's their own turf; they feel they can actually affect the outcome of a match by yelling and screaming the loudest. Football makes people feel alive. For some it's basically their whole life.'

And given that, it's not too surprising when that passion boils over.

'The violence all started in the mid 70s when the economics situation worsened,' he continued. 'It got worse through the 1980s and then in the 90s it was terrible – you know, they were carrying these long knives, they were shooting each other, having wars in parks and fights outside the stadiums...'

'And now?' asked Danny.

'Now it's not so bad... Because it's such a nice stadium here the fans want to protect it, and there is such a nice feeling here and the club wants to fill the stadiums up with all the well-behaved fans. But the violent passion is always there. Things spark up all the time.'

'And what about weapons? Are they still a big thing here?'

'You can't take anything into the stadium,' he said, 'but outside the stadium you can expect things like that.' He shrugged. 'On derby day, anything can happen.

'Last year when Galatasaray came here, some arrived with knives and one even came with a gun. He was caught by the fans and almost beaten to death. The guys handed him over to the police in a coma.'

The firms are known officially as 'fanatical supporter groups'. Fenerbahce's top fanatical supporter group are called KFY, standing for Kill For You.

It was Kill For You that we would be meeting after we had finished with Paul – and it was Kill For You we would be going to the derby with, right in the heart of their terrace, as deep into their territory as it gets.

'I've got to say,' said Danny. 'It's not a name I'm particularly loving.'

'Officially they will basically deny what the letters stand for,' said Paul, 'they turn the letters into something else because they don't want to be seen as violent... but they have a violent passion, which can turn into violence. And they are basically the engine of the chanting in the stadium.'

THE REAL FOOTBALL FACTORIES

'I've got to admit to you Paul,' said Danny, 'we've been doing a lot of travelling and this is the one place that I've been a bit worried about – and it's probably because of the two Brits that were stabbed here. Is it fair that I say that because of that, that the Brits maybe feel there is this rivalry between the Turkey and England? A bit of bad blood?'

Paul shrugged. 'Actually, no,' he said, 'there is not much rivalry now, and that stabbing: it was at the height of the fan warfare, back in 2000. And you know what that was about, you know what happened there? When the British moon at us it's seen as a huge insult in Turkey...'

'So that is what it was down to?' said Danny.

'Yeah that is what it was down to. Mooning.'

'So someone flashed their bum and they...'

'They died for it,' finished Paul. 'I know in England it's not a big deal – but insult the wrong person here and they will kill you. It's not about hatred for the British, it was just an isolated incident. Turkish fans are worse to each other than they are to strangers.'

We didn't know what to think. We made our excuses and left.

Kill For You of Fenerbahce – 'We are not dogs to be leashed, you know...'

Kill For You are Fenerbahce's best known firm, but they're also a pretty secretive organization. Turkey may contain some of the fiercest hooligans in world football, but, for all their viciousness in the flesh, they tend not to shout too loudly about it to the press. They let their actions do the talking. None of their boys had ever spoken to the media before.

We had arranged to meet two of their number in the back

room of a bar near the stadium. As we were shown through, they were waiting, sitting against a backdrop of yellow and blue curtains and propped-up posters of top Fener players. It looked for all the world like the kind of set-up you get when a club announces a new signing, like they were conducting a press conference.

The men themselves reinforced that impression. One of them wore jeans and a football top – he looked young, fit, able to handle himself. The other was older, a little bit thicker-set; he reclined in his chair in a silver-grey suit with open-necked shirt; he appeared less like a hooligan and more like an 80s TV cop.

The look in their eyes was familiar, however. They were appraising us from the minute we walked in, checking us out, sizing us up, deciding what to tell us and how to handle us. There wasn't much pity in those eyes.

They were introduced as Selahattin and Volkan – and as Danny strode forward with his hand stuck out as usual, all smiles and 'how you doing?', they remained seated, nodded in reply to his greetings. One of them talked fast into a mobile phone before snapping it shut.

'So,' he said. 'Let's begin.'

Danny kicked off with an easy one – asking why they followed Fenerbahce.

The older one, Volkan, spoke first: 'For me it is life,' he said. 'It's an escape from everything. It's love.'

'I can go on for hours about the meaning of being a Fenerbahce fan,' interrupted Selahattin, 'but I will just give you one example: it is more than a national pride, more than a religious belief. Fenerbahce passion is the most important thing in our lives. I am not just saying it to make myself look more fanatical than anyone else but it really is everything to us. We live Fenerbahce 24/7. It's in our veins.'

Peter asked why they chose to call their firm Kill For You.

Volkan sighed in exasperation. 'It started with a joke,' he said, which wasn't exactly the answer we were expecting. 'You know, Galatasaray, our big rival, their fans had this huge banner with "Die for you" written on it... so we only thought that if they're prepared to die for Galatasaray, who can kill them?

'So we made a banner saying "Kill for You", only as a joke, as a slogan... but the slogan remained. Everybody started calling us the Kill For You boys. We didn't kill anybody, it is only a joke.'

Selahattin spread his arms wide. 'Nowadays we only use the initials KFY,' he said, 'because the name Kill For You attracts too much attention and too much misunderstanding.'

Stan started to point out how, given recent history, it would be a pretty easy misunderstanding to make, but Peter silenced him with a look. Danny stuck to the safer topic of their cross-town rivalry.

'Personally,' said Selahattin, 'my love for Fenerbahce is much stronger then my hate for Galatasaray... if you hate the enemy more then you love your home team then there is something wrong with you.'

Danny asked him how far he's taken that hate in the past.

He thought for a minute, and then smiled. 'Well 10 years ago I had friends from University who were Galatasaray fans and we were at a derby match – me in the Fenerbahce end, them with their Galatasaray friends; and I could see them perfectly in their terrace... and so I lit a flare and I threw it over the stands, straight at my friends, you know....

'It landed right among them – I could have burnt them, they could have lost an eye – but I did not think of that. I only thought how they were the enemy. That's what happens: there is no oxygen going to the brain, you know? You can really go blind with hate sometimes... can you imagine? These were guys I studied with, I hung around with them, we did all sort of things, we got in trouble together supporting Turkey abroad – but as soon as it's Fenerbahce versus Galatasaray I forgot all about our friendship and brotherhood: I tried to burn them.'

Volkan insisted, however, that the worst of the violence was now in the past. 'It used to be that from night to morning you can fight with Galatasaray fans and police,' he said, 'but then it became too dangerous, too many people were injured and maybe died. People began to use Molotov cocktails, guns, big knives...'

Danny asked him about knife culture. 'How common is it to carry a blade here?' he wanted to know. 'Do most football fans carry knives?'

Selahattin shook his head. 'It's not just football. Knife culture is Turkish culture. In any situation in Turkey people use knives. Two guys can start fighting and it can be over anything and knives start talking.

'As for football...' he continued, 'they say there is big hooliganism in Turkey but they don't know what it was like 10 years ago. People used to burn each other. I saw it with my own eyes – people would be throwing buckets of Molotov cocktails around.'

These days, although the atmosphere inside the stadiums is more hostile than anything we're used to, it's rare for matches to be disrupted by crowd trouble. Tightened security and ruthless policing – including liberal use of tear gas and pepper spray – have seen to that.

In fact, so supposedly lawful are Kill For You these days, the firm even hold season tickets. Of course, as we would find out for ourselves, the season ticket section of the Fenerbahce ground is a little bit different from the Premiership equivalent…

'It was a group decision to buy season tickets,' said Selahattin. 'I guess it's a contribution to the club. Even though I am against this growing corporate side of football. I think the romance of football is getting lost, you know?'

Danny perked up. This was beginning to sound all-too familiar, almost British. He asked if Turkish football was going the way of the Premiership, if terrace culture was being lost in favour of clubs chasing money.

There was silence for a minute, before Volkan shrugged. 'The powers say it's progress, it's globalization,' he said. 'We try to say how this is our club – and the chairman tells us we have to be more like English fans. He says we have to sit and clap, we have to sit, not stand up, we can't use flares, can't use anything… Our chairman tells us: "be like the English"! But we are Mediterranean people! We are…'

'Hot blooded,' finished Selahattin.

'We're like the Italians,' continued Volkan. 'We have a fire in us.'

Selahattin grinned. 'We are not dogs to be leashed, you know,' he said.

Perhaps the most striking example of how different the Turkish fans are from the British came in 1996 when Graeme Souness, then manager of Galatasaray, planted a large flag in the centre circle of Fenerbahce's stadium, following his team's victory in the Turkish cup.

It was a spectacular misjudgement – and Souness almost paid for it with his life. As the Fenerbahce crowd exploded in rage, fences were torn down and the pitch was charged: the Scotsman had to run for his life, escorted from the pitch, the ground, and ultimately the city by the police.

The riots continued for days afterwards.

'It was a very stupid thing to do,' said Selahattin. 'What was he thinking? He really had to run for his life...'

Danny asked if they'd forgiven him yet.

'Oh we love Souness,' said Volkan, with a slow smile. 'We want to see him again to tell him so. You tell him from us, we'd love to see him.'

Selahattin wasn't smiling. 'I definitely I want to see him again,' he said.

• • •

Graeme Souness couldn't have got it more wrong when he planted that flag. They are quick to take offence here – and when they do consider themselves insulted, they can go to incredible lengths to redress the balance, restore some pride.

In Souness' case, the following season a Fenerbahce fan hid himself in the hoardings of the Ali Sami Yen stadium the night before the derby game – and as it kicked off ran on to the pitch with a hunting knife and a flag of his own.

He kept everyone off him for long enough to plant his own flag and restore his team's honour – but he paid for it. He 'disappeared' for a while after that – and when he reappeared he was missing an ear. They call him 'Rambo' now – partly because of his hunting knife, partly because he's seen as indestructible, partly because he's clearly a fucking lunatic.

But Souness was not the first British man to misjudge the Turkish fans – and, tragically, he would not be the last.

The history of footballing enmity between ourselves and the Turks goes back to the early 1990s – and Galatasaray's Champions League clash with Man United. If it was the first time many in Britain had heard of the Turkish club, it was a rude awakening for both players and fans alike.

The team surprised most of Old Trafford by putting three past Manchester United in the first leg of their match, with the home side rallying to make the final score 3-3; but it was the return fixture that really announced to the world just what Turkish terrace culture is all about.

'Welcome to Hell' said the banners in the stadium, and it looked like Hell, too, a seething, boiling cauldron of noise and colour and naked passion. And as thousands of flares and firecrackers burned and the noise reached deafening levels, tempers both on and off the pitch reached breaking point.

Death threats before the match had been made against Peter Schmeichel and Eric Cantona and throughout the game the fiery Frenchman was subjected to a barrage of abuse every time he got near the ball. When the game ended scoreless and United went out on the away goals rule, he snapped.

Kicking out at the Turkish bench, he took his arguments to the referee and, as the pitch seemed to fill with people celebrating, Cantona was shown a red card and bundled away. Worse was to follow – there were scuffles in the tunnel, reports that riot police had attacked the English team with batons, that some of the United players had fought back.

The team coach was stoned as it left the ground, with a window shattering above Steve Bruce's head.

Meanwhile, a United fans' hotel was attacked, the lobby

bricked and supporters stoned. Many of the Englishmen then clashed with the same police that had been called to rescue them: they were dragged off and thrown in jail.

Naturally, packs of the remaining United boys firmed up and retaliated in kind – but many did not, and there were reports of fans being herded up and imprisoned just for wearing the wrong shirts. Over 170 of them were later deported and it took the authorities months to rescue others from Istanbul jails.

The warnings were there. But either nobody was paying attention, or everyone was still underestimating the lengths to which the Istanbul firms will go. In April 2000 things came to a bloody head.

Taksim Square, in the European half of the city, is a busy, bustling, cosmopolitan area now. In the heart of Istanbul's entertainment district, it's filled with shops, bars, stalls selling souvenirs and tat, people hurrying to and fro or else sitting chilling out... it's like any other city centre square. It's like Leicester Square, or Princes Street, or Piccadilly Gardens.

We went to see the place for ourselves. None of us had been here before but it all felt oddly, spookily, familiar. Walking around now, landmarks from the newsreels still stand out. There's the McDonald's, there's the bars, the places still recognisable in the clear daylight from the shaky, panicked news footage of that dark night in 2000.

'Difficult to imagine now,' said Stan, as we watched flocks of pigeons take off and land, pecking among shoppers and tourists for scraps.

We walked around in silence, trying to picture how it must have been. This is a place, after all, more used to celebration. It was here that the authorities put up big screens for the

THE REAL FOOTBALL FACTORIES

World Cup matches, here that massive crowds gathered to watch Turkey's 2002 semi-final against Brazil. There was music, fireworks, balloons and a stage show that night. But two years earlier there had been blood on the pavement.

When Galatasaray drew Leeds in the UEFA cup semi-final, the portents were there. Since Man United's fiery visit to Turkey seven years earlier the two countries had continued a tempestuous relationship on and off the pitch – and the previous year Chelsea had endured similarly hostile scenes when they visited for a European match.

What nobody predicted, however, was just how far things would go.

Some 500 Leeds fans made the trip to Turkey – and rather than being organized mobs, they were for the most part just ordinary supporters, albeit in typical British-abroad high-spirits. It was this cultural gulf – and not any of the 'usual' hooligan trouble – that was to prove the catalyst for tragedy.

The English fans congregated around Taksim Square – close to the ground, it's also where most of the bars and fast-food joints are to be found. As night fell and the beers kicked in there was singing, taunting. Gangs of Galatasaray fans started showing up, angry knots of boys not appreciating the mocking chants of the visiting fans.

Some of the Leeds support got a little too boisterous for the locals. There are suggestions that 'improper' remarks were made to local girls. There was mooning, the kind of thing you'd see in any British town centre on a Saturday night, fat boys with their jeans round their knees, arses out for the lads.

Except that over here, mooning is seen as a massive insult. A proper insult. The kind of insult that, according to ancient Turkish traditions of pride and honour, demands revenge. It has been reported that some of the English lads went further, started ripping up banknotes, defacing images of Kemal Ataturk. The locals exploded.

The news footage of that night captures the panic and chaos – Leeds fans stumbling, confused around McDonald's and outside the bars, packs of locals swift and brutal among them. Flashpoints of violence, the police wading in with batons, suddenly blood, screaming, fallen bodies...

Leeds fans have spoken since of the trouble erupting out of nowhere, of Galatasaray fans streaming out of shops and bars armed with bottles, iron bars, knives; of being chased, hunted down, by packs of up to 50 men... of the escalation in violence being sudden, unexpected, and devastating.

In the midst of it all were Christopher Loftus and Kevin Speight, two Leeds fans who really had just come to see their team play in the semis of the UEFA Cup. Both in their late thirties, they were unknown to the British authorities, neither had ever been in trouble before.

Christopher Loftus was stabbed 17 times in the heart and pronounced dead shortly after arriving in hospital. Kevin Speight was stabbed six times and died in the operating theatre. Five other Leeds fans were seriously injured.

As we heard the news in horror back in England, the reaction in Turkey spoke volumes about how society works here. Some of the papers almost suggested that the provocation justified the killings: 'It's as if they came for a fight,' headlined the daily *Milliyet*. There was not an abundance of sympathy for the dead Englishmen.

The game went ahead anyway: there was not even an official minute's silence.

We stood ourselves, quiet in the midst of the busy, bustling square, watching the bars fill up. Excited chatter, shouting, laughter carried over to us.

None of us really fancied a drink here; we turned in silence and left. Tomorrow we'd be back to meet Galatasaray's top firm.

• • •

If you've never been woken up with a hangover by the Muslim call to prayer, count yourself lucky. Or at least, count yourself lucky if it's never happened to you at whatever godforsaken time in the morning it blared across the city and into our hotel rooms. The amplified wail woke us all up, sent us to breakfast bleary-eyed and already jumpy.

'I'm gonna be honest with you,' said Danny, pouring himself one of the lethal local coffees. 'I've hit a dip. Eight countries in ten weeks; it's starting to take its toll, running around talking to naughty people. I feel battered.' He took a sip and grimaced. 'Look at the state of me, look at me boat. Look, the culmination of all these countries, the dangerous people...'

Stan nodded in silent agreement. We were all knackered, all running on fumes – and our adventure in Istanbul was about to take a frightening twist.

Today was the day of the big derby. We were going to get ourselves back to Galatasaray's manor in the morning to hook up with the top boys of top firm UltrAslan – and then race back across the city to meet their deadly rivals from KFY. We'd be watching the game in the heart of Kill For You's stand – and what we really didn't want to happen was for either firm to suss that we'd been hanging out with the other.

It was a tight schedule. Tighter than we realized.

The UltrAslan of Galatasaray – 'If anyone challenges us then we will do what ever it takes – put a cat in a corner and you could get your face scratched up...'

Kick off that night was scheduled for seven – but the doors to Fener's Sukru Saracoglu stadium were going to open at three: for a match like this it's not unusual to find the ground packed and in full voice for at least three hours before kick off.

We pitched up in Taksim Square at midday and made our way down to the Ali Sami Yen. The cosmopolitan bustle of the previous day had been replaced by a tenser, quieter, atmosphere. It felt like the city was holding its breath.

As we approached the stadium we couldn't help but notice the groups of lads in red shirts hanging about; there were little gangs of five or six on every corner... and they noticed us too. We became conscious of being followed.

'It's cool,' said Peter. 'The geezer we're meeting: he calls himself Alpaslan and he's a serious boy here, he commands respect. No one's going to give us any grief once they know he's on our side.'

We reached our rendezvous spot and stopped, turned around, looked about. Stan shifted from one foot to the other, holding his camera tripod in one hand and watching the lads around us carefully.

A couple of Galatasaray lads strolled past, all grins and swagger. They clocked us and started to chant: 'UltrAslan! UltrAslan!'

'This is the firm we're meeting, right?' said Danny. 'Anyone else feeling a bit diggy, a bit nervous? Everywhere I am looking there's people knocking about and a lot have got a naughty look about them, I must say...'

He turned to the lads nearest us, the ones singing. 'You sweet, boys? You sweet?'

They looked confused for a second – and then were distracted by a commotion behind them. It was Alpaslan, our man, top boy of this outfit.

A big lug he was too. Six foot tall and built like he was pushing 15 stone at least, he walked towards us flanked by two deputies, all in black, and a growing mob of red-shirted, singing Galatasaray boys. His head was shaved, his hands were massive and he had the familiar look in his eyes – the look we'd seen in more than one top boy we'd talked to. It's a look of supreme confidence and also of total pitilessness. It was obvious that Alpaslan was not a man to be messed with... and it was clear he would go to whatever lengths were necessary for his outfit, that he wouldn't stop until the job was done.

By the time he reached us his little band of followers had grown to about 20. He gave us a big grin, shook our hands, kissed Danny on both cheeks. 'Welcome,' he said.

'Not at all, not at all, lovely to meet you,' said Danny with the usual charm. 'Thank you for talking to me,' he looked around as Stan hurriedly set up. 'So all the Galatasaray boys are here then... big day for you lads, is it? Looking forward to the match?'

'Well between Galatasaray and Fenerbahce there is over 100 years of rivalry,' said Alpaslan, slowly, 'but there are no obvious reasons for the hatred between us.' He grinned. 'We don't need reasons. Maybe the reason is simply that we are all a bit stupid.

'As for today's game – now you can see here that a lot of our friends are excited. I can guarantee you that a lot of them have been out all last night and they did not sleep – they all had a sleepless night. We only have 2,500 seats in their ground today but we think we are going to be stronger because our 2,500 men are the soldiers – they are men that cannot be silenced.'

'So is it likely to be dangerous?'

He shook his head. 'I don't think it is going to be too dangerous for you today,' and he looked us all up and down and smiled again. 'But if you asked me this question 15 or 20 years ago I would tell you that it's very, very dangerous...'

Behind him the firm members started chanting again: 'UltrAslan! UltrAslan!' As Stan trained the camera on them they began jumping around, po-going and gurning and mugging for the lens. One of them kept still, however. He had a hood drawn tight over his face, obscuring everything but his eyes, and in his hand he held a flag. Amid the noise and movement around him, he stared straight at Stan.

Peter glanced at Stan to see if he'd noticed. He had, but he'd swung the camera back to Danny, who had just asked Alpaslan if he had anything to say to the Fenerbahce fans.

'What message I would give to them? I would say to be clever,' he said, to clapping and cheering from the boys behind him. ' Wherever Galatasaray go we will support them all the way...'

'And what if they're not clever? What if they attack you?'

Alpaslan flexed his massive shoulders. 'If anyone challenges us then we will do whatever it takes – put a cat in a corner and you could get your face scratched up...' His boys started clapping again. 'Only we are not cats,' he continued. 'We are lions and we will show our true nature.'

More lads were wandering over, attracted by the cheering

and the cameras, eager to see what was happening. By now there was quite a crowd and Peter was getting nervous. He signalled to get a move on and Danny cut to the chase.

'So then,' he said, 'can you tell us what happened with the Leeds incident? 'Cos in England we have one story, you know... but we'd like to hear the other side of the story. What's your opinion?'

The crowd went quiet and Alpaslan sighed and then frowned. He leaned forward. 'I will explain to you,' he said. 'I have been to many matches in Europe and in every country I've been we respect the culture, the flag, the women and the children. We have never been involved in insulting the country or its culture. And likewise, when rival teams have come to Turkey – the Italians, Spanish, Manchester United, Real Madrid and other countries – they have come here and there has never been any problems with them, we swapped shirts, drank together, ate together and enjoyed each other's company.

'But when Leeds came that time they were very rude and insulting. They defaced our flag, they defaced pictures of Ataturk and they ripped up our money... and in the Taksim area they drank too much and they made local people feel very uncomfortable and insulted.

'You have to understand that is the area of Galatasaray where the club and the college is, it's the main hub for Galatasaray and when the local people heard that this kind of behaviour was going on, they came on to the streets... and unfortunately things happened that we didn't want to happen.'

He shrugged. 'But I am afraid they did happen. We were very upset... but it happened and there is nothing else we can do about it.'

'Okay...' started Danny, even as Peter frowned, but

Alpaslan hadn't finished. Behind him his crew were silent, listening intently.

'I am afraid that even after the match, the Leeds supporters – despite what had happened – still behaved in the same manner as before, they were still insulting and disrespectful.' He sighed. 'But nothing else happened, thankfully. We calmed the people down.'

There was sporadic applause behind him again, and everyone seemed satisfied with this version of events. Danny shot Peter a look, thought better of arguing the point, and instead stuck out his hand. 'Thanks once again for speaking to us,' he said. 'Really appreciate it. Good of you.'

'Okay,' said Alpaslan, checking his watch. 'We're good then, yes?' And without waiting for an answer, he strode off.

We should have left with him – but Stan wanted to get some more shots of the UltrAslan lads singing and chanting and mobbing up while we were here. He had the idea of filming some impromptu interviews with some of them and we were setting up when a beer can came arcing through the sky and exploded at his feet.

'What the fuck…' he began. We looked up straight at a knot of lads staring right back at us, daring us to react.

'Not good,' muttered Peter, and a bottle zipped through the air, whistling past his ear and smashing into the pavement behind us.

Stan snapped his camera off and we weighed up our chances. All we could think of was to run.

But running wasn't an option. There was nowhere to run, we were deep in the Galatasaray manor, right outside their stadium, for Christ's sake. The only people around were wearing red shirts and singing UltrAslan songs. We could maybe make it as far as the busier Taksim Square but of course we knew that that place didn't exactly have a reputation as a safe haven.

None of us wanted to say it, but as Stan hefted his tripod up again we all knew that if it came down to it, we only had one choice. And the best we could hope for was to not get hurt too badly.

'Right...' started Stan, and then suddenly one of Alpaslan's big deputies was behind us, hands on our shoulders. 'Time for you to go now,' he said with a frown, and practically picked up Stan as he shepherded us quickly through the middle of the little mob that had assembled around us and into a waiting cab. The backs of our necks prickled as we hurried away – every one of us braced for the inevitable smack on the back of the head, the rush of pain and blood... but it never came.

'My advice to you is – don't come back,' said our unlikely saviour. We didn't need telling twice.

We later heard that someone had in fact called the police and they showed up not long after our escape. We also heard that an off-duty copper had been stabbed just around the corner... because he was wearing a Fenerbahce shirt.

We raced back to the Fener side of the city ahead of the Galatasaray fans. We still had a football match to go to.

Fenerbahce vs Galatasaray – 'No mercy, no fear'
We were buzzing. Buzzing? We were rushing; we were flying.

'Fuck me,' said Stan, 'fuck me. Fucking hell but... fuck me.' He shook his head, searching for the right words to express his feelings. 'Fuck me.'

'Too close,' said Peter. 'Way too close. We don't get that close again, alright?'

Danny grinned. 'I need a drink,' he said. 'I need a big fucking drink of something cold and alcoholic and then I need to go shout myself stupid at a football game. Know what I mean?'

We were meeting our lads from KFY at a bar near the stadium – but in the meantime there was an hour or so to soak up the atmosphere. We got ourselves drinks and took in the sights.

Everywhere was yellow and blue. Or at least – everywhere except the long lines of black, the riot police with their shields and batons, their helmets and their holstered cans of pepper spray. They lined the streets, content to watch for the time being, but ready for trouble.

Meanwhile, the Fenerbahce fans were in party mood. Every street seemed to hold another marching mob of them, all flags and scarves, whistles and cheers, always led by one man at the front, trooping like squadrons, like phalanxes of some ancient army – all headed for the stadium. They sang as they marched and those watching smiled and cheered along.

'This is more like it,' said Peter, and he asked a man next to us what the songs meant.

'They're singing to the Galatasaray fans,' he explained. 'They're saying: "we're going to stick our dicks in your mothers".'

Stan burst out laughing and Danny sprayed his beer everywhere. 'You fucking tell them, lads!' he shouted. He beamed at Peter. 'I've got to say man, there is nothing like the excitement of a derby day. Even when you are well out of your manor you just feel it in the air, it is a beautiful thing.'

'It is now,' said Peter. 'I don't want to be funny or anything, but I'm glad we're going to the match with this lot and not the others, know what I mean? Speaking of which...' he downed his beer and stood up. 'We've got a date to keep.'

We found the right bar and trooped in – Danny was immediately mobbed. 'Alright boys,' he grinned, 'alright brother, how are you? How's it going?' The contrast with the morning couldn't have been greater. If that was the fierce, intimidating, proud side of Turkey, this was the other side of the country's culture – welcoming, warm, friendly. We were all given drinks and, much to Stan's amusement, huge yellow and white KFY coats to wear.

'What do we look like?' he laughed, 'We look like big fucking marshmallows.'

'I'll be honest with you,' said Danny, 'you look a bit of a treacle in it son, I hope they're not mugging us off, taking the piss out of the English...'

Maybe it was the release of tension, maybe it was the adrenaline, or maybe we weren't used to Turkish beer, but by the time we got to the match we were half-slaughtered. Mints were passed round – and it was explained that the police would not let anyone in whom they suspected of being drunk.

Somehow we got in anyway.

Inside the stadium was pandemonium. Fifty thousand people were jumping up and down simultaneously. The roar was like sticking your head into a waterfall, or a tsunami, or an avalanche; the whole place shook with the power of it.

We squeezed through the terraces to our spot in the heart of the season ticket area, in the middle of the Kill For You section, where every member of the firm spent every home match. Our new marshmallow coats earned us slaps on the back and kisses on the cheek and more than once we were physically lifted off our feet. There were seats here but nobody was sitting. Nobody sat the whole game.

Everybody seemed to be making as much noise as they could. We shouted and sang along too – within minutes we were hoarse.

Opposite us a banner was unfurled, one of the same ones we had seen the boys laying out the day before – it felt like a lifetime ago. 'No mercy, no fear,' it read. The stadium roared and suddenly above our heads our own banner was laid out and we were engulfed in a tent as thousands of hands held it up and a matching roar greeted us from the other end.

'Where's Galatasaray?' shouted Danny, and Stan pointed to a terrace below us and to our left. It was covered in netting – protection against coins and rocks and whatever else could be thrown – but was nonetheless subject to an onslaught of taunts, a ceaseless barrage of abuse.

To be fair, for their part, the boys of UltrAslan gave as good as they got – the 2,500 that Alpaslan had brought to the Sukru Saracoglu were on their feet, looking from where we were like furious beetles waving and gesticulating at the monstrous crowds around them.

The game kicked off and somehow the noise got even louder. The intensity was the equal of anything we'd seen around the world – a constant, ear-splitting din of chanting and roaring, sirens and horns... and whenever Galatasaray got the ball the volume increased to fever pitch, a pandemonium of whistles and jeers; the sound of sheer, naked hate.

'We are so far out of our manor it's not even funny,' shouted Danny, and before Stan could answer all hell broke loose.

Fenerbahce had scored and the place blew up, the whole

stadium jumping and hugging and throwing themselves around like madmen. A man in front of us climbed on his mate's shoulders and hurled himself face forward down the terraces... he surfed the crowd down as far as we could follow.

And we jumped and shouted and celebrated with them – there was nothing to do but give in and go with it.

Unbelievably, minutes later Fener scored again. The celebrations were doubled, trebled. It was mayhem. Nearly 50,000 people in yellow and blue all losing it, all at the same time.

All, that is, except for the angry little mass of red in the stand below us. As the rest of the stadium went apeshit, they stood dead still. And then slowly, deliberately, a seat was ripped out, lobbed towards the fence. And then another.

The mood changed immediately. Sections of the crowd – ours included – turned their attention from the pitch towards the Galatasaray supporters.

At half time the police charged in and we watched as the visitors met the truncheons and the pepper spray full on. They were still fighting when the second half began and the locals were getting restless. Unable to get to the men who were tearing up their stadium, they turned their attention back to the Galatasaray team. The visiting goalkeeper was pelted; a firework spiralled down and missed his head by inches.

Things were on a knife-edge. On the one hand the visiting fans were damaging the Fenerbahce boys' beloved home ground... on the other, the last thing they wanted to do was get the game called off when they were 2-0 up. The KFY boys in our end weren't happy. They would rather win the match and deal with the troublemakers later. The word was passed. Things calmed down and the game continued.

By final whistle Galatasaray had pulled one back and their fans were distracted long enough by the goal for the police to storm their end and restore a bit of order.

As they were escorted from the ground, everyone else stayed put, arms around each other, singing something joyous and probably obscene about another famous derby victory.

We were on our last legs. We kept it together long enough to get out of the stadium and back to our hotel… and then we crashed. The next day we were on another plane.

'Never in my life,' said Danny as we quit Turkey. He looked done in. We all did. 'Never in all my fucking life…'

CHAPTER NINE

ITALY

World Cup winners one week, engulfed in corruption scandals the next. Football in Italy is an opera. And football support here is no less dramatic, full of fire and passion and love and pain.

Oh – and death.

When English and Italian firms clashed in the 1980s, modern international hooliganism was born – and lived its most infamous hour. Even as the events of Heysel and beyond saw the authorities crack down on English terrace culture, it inspired a whole new way of support over here. The Ultras of Italy see themselves as modern day gladiators. They have made football hooliganism an all-consuming passion… but it comes at a terrible price.

We were here to meet men from Turin who still nurse deep wounds – and who aren't prepared to either forgive or to forget what happened at Heysel. And if we got through that unscathed, we were off to the most explosive derby in Europe – Roma v Lazio in the Stadio Olimpico.

We were in Italy just before things got deadly again, just before the authorities finally declared war on the gladiators of the terraces, just before policemen started getting killed.

We were going out with a bang.

It's not over till the fat lady sings.

Italy. Home of passion, culture, art, opera, architecture, seat of the Roman Empire, the Catholic Church... and birthplace of the Ultras, the fiercest, best-organized, most passionate, most political, most powerful football firms in the world.

The summer before our visit, the country had been rocked by the biggest corruption scandal in the history of the game. And then they won the World Cup. Perfect. *Bellezza e la Bestia*, as they say over here. Beauty and the Beast.

God, we couldn't wait to get to Italy!

From the very beginning it felt in a funny way like everything was leading us here. We'd been right around the world... but we were always going to end up in Italy. Sure, you've got the heat, colour and insanity of South America, you've got the cold brutality and remorseless hatred of Eastern Europe – and we'd seen both extremes a little too close for comfort on this trip – but Italy is still the benchmark of the international scene. On and off the pitch.

In many ways, this is where international football hooliganism was born. Believe it or not, the Italians had a hand in defining the most famous English firms of the 1970s and 80s. The boys from the Thames and the Mersey and the Tyne came here, and when they weren't tearing up the terraces and trashing the town squares, they were busy storming the shopping arcades – kitting themselves out in the latest Italian threads.

THE REAL FOOTBALL FACTORIES

The look of our terraces was made in Italy. Before those famous European campaigns we were stomping about in boots and bomber jackets... after a few visits here our firms began to cut a dash in more casual threads.

It wasn't a totally one-way street, of course. The Italians soaked up a bit of our culture too. They learned fast. They combined their wholehearted love of the beautiful game with a territorial passion magnified in intensity by their hot Mediterranean blood... and they soon found that there's a fine line between passion and naked violence.

It was in Italy that the Ultras first appeared. The modern face of football support, they encompass all the most extreme elements of terrace culture, from the joyous, jaw-dropping beauty of mass choreography to the sickening, stinking reality of murder.

If England is the birthplace of football hooliganism, Italy can lay claim to being its modern home. And it was when English and Italian firms came together one bloody night in Heysel, Belgium, that football hooliganism was brought to the attention of the world. Nothing has been the same since.

● ● ●

'Bellisimo!' whistled Stan, probably incomprehensibly to the locals. 'Bella, bella! La Dolce Vita!'

His camera followed two girls as they swung past in the sunshine, all hips and bare legs, brown skin and smooth, rolling steps... before his attention was distracted by another pair – their laughter carried across the Piazza Navona to where we sat sipping coffee in one of the cafes.

'It's no good,' said Stan, eventually. 'It's impossible to

concentrate. I see the most beautiful girl in the world... and then a minute later I see someone even more beautiful. And then...' he trailed off as a girl who looked like Angelina Jolie sat at the table next to us, placed a filterless cigarette between blood red lips and accepted a light off the waiter. 'Mama Mia. I'm in love.'

He turned the camera off, admitted defeat.

Everywhere we looked, everything was beautiful. The girls were beautiful, the fountains in the square were beautiful, the buildings surrounding the square were beautiful. Even our drinks looked beautiful – the espressos small but perfectly formed, rich black against the smooth white porcelain cups.

In fact, when all was said and done, we were probably the only things around here that weren't beautiful. We'd been in Italy a few hours and we were already in love with the place.

Of course, we hadn't seen the flipside yet; we hadn't met the beast. But we would.

We would find ourselves cornered in a bar in Turin with lurid images from *A Clockwork Orange* on the walls while a man jabbed his finger at us like a knife and explained in no uncertain terms exactly why he hates all Englishmen...

We would find ourselves in the heart of the fascist terraces with the two most fearsome firms in Italy – and we'd play ourselves off between them, slipping from one to the other, even as the stadium shook around us.

We would feel terror and adrenaline and the lurch of pure fear... and because this is Italy we'd also feel uplifted, inspired, and the rush of pure joy.

In the town of Bergamo in the foothills of the Alps, we would meet a man who looked like Jesus – and he would explain to us why, for his firm, violence is an almost evangelical pursuit. And why, when they kick the shit out of each other, they are really maintaining the true spirit of the game.

'Football as it stands today, it's disgusting,' he told us. 'But there are those like us who still maintain and pass on the real passion of the game. The fight is the ultimate conclusion of what we're about, it's the most beautiful thing we can do – because it is the one really determined by our hearts.'

For the moment, however, we were in Rome. And Stan was collecting footage of hot Italian chicks walking through the square.

'That film's expensive,' pointed out Peter, 'we're supposed to be using it for something other than your sordid private collection. We're here to shoot big nasty Ultra boys, remember.'

The only problem was – we were having a little difficulty getting any of them to talk to us. We'd spent a few days kicking around the sights, soaking up the atmosphere and eating a lot of spaghetti... but we hadn't managed to infiltrate the firms here. The Lazio v Roma derby was coming up fast and we needed a way in.

And then someone had the bright idea of asking one of our boys on the ground here what team he supports. Turns out he only used to run with the Juventus Ultras...

Fabiano the Fixer – 'It's a strong, deep passion; an insane passion. You can't be an Ultra unless you are insane'
In every country we visited on this trip we had 'fixers' – local boys whose job it was to help us out, sort us out... and get us in and out of wherever we needed to go. We couldn't have done it without them – some of these fixers had been negotiating with the firms in their countries for weeks before

our arrival, trying to balance our needs with their concerns about secrecy, security, and so on.

Mostly they were journalists, or people involved in sport – and most of the time the fact that we were a British TV crew and that one of us was the star of *The Football Factory* was enough to get us access. Every now and then, of course, we ran up against a brick wall – and then it was down to the fixers to see what strings they could pull, what favours they could call in.

This was one of those times.

Our fixer out here was Fabiano – tall, handsome, with a shaved head and a little moustache, he looked a bit like a young Gianluca Vialli. He'd been trying to sort us out with access to the Ultras and none of the usual tricks were working. They didn't care that we were English – if anything it counted against us – and they didn't care that we were going to put them on TV. And, most annoying of all, they didn't care about Danny. They didn't care about *The Football Factory* any more than they cared about *Finding Nemo*. (In fact, if we could have promised them a meeting with the star of *Finding Nemo*, they'd probably have been a lot more up for it.)

Fabiano had to try something else.

He's a clean boy now, doesn't get himself into any trouble at all... but our Fab was once part of one of the most respected Ultras groups in Italy. As a young man he followed Juve – and he still had enough clout with the lads in Turin to pull some strings for us.

We met him by the most famous stadium in Rome to find out just what being an Ultra means.

'This ain't bad at all,' said Danny, as we strolled round the Colosseum. The massive arches still looked capable of supporting the weight of 50-odd thousand screaming fans;

the 2,000-year-old pillars and podiums and columns worn but still solid, ingrained with the sweat and blood of 500 years of sport and slaughter.

'This is where it all used to go off proper style,' said Stan, 'chariot races, gladiators, Christians v Lions. Must have been fucking amazing.'

'I've just had a thought,' said Danny, brightly. 'They should reopen this, chuck a few different firms in there, let them have a big tear up. No weapons, obviously. I'm sure people will come and pay to watch that, keep it in a nice safe environment… you could even have a World Cup – all the different nationalities having a right tear up in there.'

We all started laughing and he looked confused. 'What are you laughing about?' he said. 'I'm serious. Think about it.'

'Think about the TV rights,' said Peter.

'Exactly,' he said. 'It's genius.'

Fabiano arrived and Peter found us a nice scenic spot for the interview. Behind us, tourists picked their way through the ancient stones, as Fab explained just what being an Ultra means.

'The word Ultra in Italian derives from '*oltre*', which means 'beyond' – as in beyond the limit. So being an Ultra means being prepared to go beyond the limit for your team. It means trying to be the best, always trying to be one step above everybody else. An Ultra always goes beyond the limit.'

'So it's a passion thing,' asked Danny, 'an expression of passion?'

'Oh yes, it's a strong, deep passion; an insane passion. You can't be an Ultra unless you are insane, really. If you're not insane, you're not going beyond, you're not Ultra.'

He asked him if the Ultras stoked that passion with alcohol. Fab shook his head.

'No, that's a difference between English and Italian,' he said. 'I drink, I like to drink, but I never drink before a match. Nobody is drunk. Everybody has to be clear-headed, ready; because we've got strategies, tactics and a lot of things to think about during a game. Just to prepare for one important game can take months.'

We knew that the Ultras were not all about violence, that their displays – their choreography, putting on a show for the opposition – were an integral part of their makeup... but we wanted to know just how important the violence was too.

Fab shrugged. 'Ultras don't think about what is important, we just think about who we are, the flag we represent,' he explained. 'If we go to a game you have to demonstrate that you are the best. How do you do that? You have two choices. Singing, support for 90 minutes, fireworks and everything...

'But more important is how much stronger physically you are than your rivals. You do whatever it takes. The hate is so strong. For example, the Italian national team is not followed at all by hooligans, because nobody could stand in the same terraces, the hate is so strong.'

He explained that this intense pride was part of the reason why the firms were not impressed by our media credentials. 'They don't like the media at all,' he said. 'The media is just a way to sell programmes and newspapers. Ultras are proud: they live life their way.'

Nevertheless, Fabiano's name was still solid enough with the Juventus Ultras for their most notorious firm to make an exception, break their silence. It was especially remarkable because round those parts no one is hated quite like the English are hated.

Fab had got us in – the only question was whether it was into a place we really wanted to go.

• • •

Turin is in the far northwest of Italy, in the shadows of the Alps and only about 50 miles from the French border. It's a city known for its culture, its history – it was the capital of Italy at one point – and also for its industry, with Fiat's headquarters here.

The natives reflect that mix – they've got the fire, the passion of artistic and cultural Italy... and they've got a hard, modern, industrial edge too. And both sides come together on the football pitch.

Juventus are the team Italians either love or hate. They're the Man United of the Mediterranean. They're the most successful club in Italy, with over 40 Italian trophies to their name, and they have supporters' clubs the length and breadth of the country.

Back home, however, they're probably best known for the events of 29 May, 1985. At the European Cup Final against Liverpool in the Heysel Stadium, Brussels, firms from both teams came together in what has become known as one of the darkest days in hooligan history.

The trouble started early. Liverpool fans had been arriving from the ferries all morning, and most had – as is traditional on European away days – hit the beers as soon as they arrived. By late afternoon the effects of the strong Belgian lager were being felt all over the city, and the riot police were beginning to make their presence felt too. Angry confrontations flashed up around Brussels town centre; at the stadium things got worse.

It's now accepted that Heysel was not a suitable venue for such a tie: the outer walls were crumbling and fans from both sides were simply climbing in through gaps or over fences. Inside, the supporters were segregated by chicken wire fencing and a thin line of Belgian riot police... as well as a 'neutral zone', section Z.

It didn't take long before the first missiles started soaring over the lines and smashing into both sets of fans – the terraces were heaving, overcrowded, the numbers swollen dangerously by the lack of proper security and the fact that people were able to simply walk in without a ticket. The rocks flew faster, harder; tensions began to rise.

About an hour before kick off a group of Liverpool fans charged the flimsy barriers separating them from the Italians – through and over the chicken wire and what police there were – into Section Z and towards the Juventus fans.

The Italians retreated and many scrambled over a perimeter wall close to the corner flag. The crumbling wall couldn't take the weight. It collapsed; and 39 people died. Thirty-two of them were Italian Juve fans.

Incredibly, the game went ahead anyway (Juve won, thanks to a Platini penalty) and officially the entire blame for the disaster was laid on the Liverpool fans. UEFA official observer Gunter Schneider said: 'Only the English fans were responsible. Of that there is no doubt.'

English clubs were banned from Europe for five years, with Liverpool serving another year on top of that. But there has never been an official enquiry.

Not that they need one in Turin. Here, their feelings are pretty clear. The graffiti near our hotel spelt it out clearly enough: 'We hate Liverpool,' it said, in blood red. 'English animals'.

More than 20 years on from Heysel, they haven't forgiven and they haven't forgotten. Fabiano explained to us that the Juventus Ultras see themselves as defenders of the fans' honour – it's almost their duty to avenge the dead of Heysel.

And we were going to meet the worst of them.

The Drughi of Juventus – 'All it takes is for anything to happen in the stadium, the slightest thing, a small spark and it's off, mayhem…'

Fabiano had sorted us out for an audience with three of the top boys of the Drughi – Juventus' most notorious Ultras group. Originally called The Black & White Supporters, they dropped the English name after Heysel, in favour of their native tongue. 'Drughi' itself is a reference to the Droogs, the gang in Stanley Kubrick's banned film *A Clockwork Orange*, for whom 'ultraviolence' – rape, robbery, assault and battery – is a way of life.

Nice lads, then.

We were told three of the Drughi – Mimmo, the leader, Fabio, who described himself as an 'organizer' and Christian, their translator – would see us in their bar that night. We weren't to come until it was dark.

We were also told to tread carefully. The Drughi have a deep hatred of the English: they had asked what teams each of us followed, and although they seemed satisfied that none of us were Scousers, they were still pretty antsy about the whole thing.

We met for a drink beforehand, a bit of Dutch Courage. Except we didn't really know what to get down us. Since pretty early in our round-the-world trip we'd been tailoring our poison to suit our location – cachaca rum in South

America, vodka in Eastern Europe, fuck-knows-what-it-was in Holland and Turkey – but we couldn't decide what was appropriate here. Red wine just seemed a bit, well, weird, given the situation.

And we also remembered what Fabiano had said about clear heads, about being ready for anything. We sat staring at a bar menu for a while before Stan spoke.

'Fuck this,' he said, 'I'm getting the beers in. Peroni – that's Italian, right?'

In 20 minutes we sank a dozen bottles of the lager between us. We were ready.

Peter had directions to the bar – but he was told he could ask anyone and they would know. We wandered down alleys and backstreets that seemed to get darker and quieter, the further on we went.

By the time we reached the right street, our hearts were hammering and each of us was chaining our cigarettes. We'd been in more intimidating places before – but we'd never gone to meet a firm so outspoken in their contempt for us before.

And there really was no one else around.

We couldn't miss the bar itself. One window was covered by the word: DRUGHI – the other obscured by a massive poster from *A Clockwork Orange*. It showed the four heroes of that film in silhouette, tooled up with sticks and knives, ready for action. It was, it turned out, this firm's official logo.

Inside, more posters covered the walls, images of bright celluloid ultraviolence mixed with shots of Juventus in action, of spectacular crowd choreographies, of stands bright with flares and fireworks.

The place was empty – aside from our three boys. They stood with their backs to the bar, arms folded. As we came in and Danny went through his usual round of handshakes and backslaps and 'alright geezer's they continued to look unimpressed.

They were older than most of the guys we'd met – Mimmo especially looked like he'd been around the block a few times, with the kind of weather-beaten skin and solid frame that you knew would take some punishment. He looked like an old tree – gnarly and knotted and hard. Danny asked him what being an Ultra meant.

'Being an Ultra is not something you can define,' he said. 'You need to feel the desire inside of you... it's not something you can just do, that someone can tell you "Come along, be an Ultra". It's something that you do for your team, or for your friends. You do it because you want to take up their fight.'

'Like a code of honour, then?'

Mimmo looked at us like we were idiots. 'No. It's not really a code of honour. It's just the law of the stadium. You go to the stadium to support the team that you love. So it is not unusual that many things can happen once you are there. If I get into trouble, if he gets into trouble, or one of the others... that's the code that keeps us together. His problem is my problem, it's like a chain that binds us.'

'So it's like a code of honour then,' muttered Stan.

Mimmo started to answer but Peter interrupted him. 'Tell us what makes the Drughi special,' he said.

Mimmo kept talking. 'What makes us special? We are a force to be reckoned with, we don't fear anyone or anything. We face things together, we share our day-to-day with each other, inside and outside of the stadium, and we just don't give a fuck about anyone.'

He took a step forward, towards Stan, his voice getting louder.

'If you are a Drughi it means you are someone who's sorted, who's tough, who doesn't mess around,' he said. He jabbed his finger in Stan's chest. 'It means you are an Ultra, you are afraid of nothing and no one, and when I say nothing I mean NOTHING. And we don't give a shit about ANYONE, alright?' He was shouting now. 'We really don't care about ANYONE, we are against EVERYTHING and EVERYONE. okay?'

Stan concentrated on his camera, avoiding Mimmo's glare. Peter swallowed.

'Okay,' laughed Danny, trying to cut the tension. 'I think I got the gist of that...'

'*Cazzo*,' spat Mimmo, and took a step back again. Both Fabio and Christian the interpreter burst out laughing.

We didn't know what it meant and we ignored it – we had to. Danny pressed on, but Peter was already surreptitiously glancing around, calculating just what our chances might be if we had to duck out suddenly. Stan kept his head down.

'How does someone become an Ultra?' asked Danny.

'Like I said before, you don't become an Ultra, you are born an Ultra,' replied Mimmo. 'First of all you need big balls. You need big balls, if you ain't got those, stay at home and don't bother the rest of us...'

He asked him if the Drughi Ultras ever used weapons.

Mimmo considered for a moment. 'You can't really generalize about that sort of thing,' he said. 'Sometimes a good punch is better than a crowbar to the head; being hit with a stick is not as bad as getting a proper kick. It's just something that you do in the moment. You don't decide in advance... we don't take anything with us. All the Ultra really needs are these,' he held up his hands, 'and these,' and he grabbed his balls.

He grinned and continued, a little calmer now, getting into his stride. 'As far as the Ultras code goes, there's no such thing as using a blade or a handgun. None of that. Punches, man to man combat, if you beat me I take it, if I beat you, you take it. Understood? *Capite*? At any rate, we're ready for everyone and anyone, we don't fear anybody.'

The other man, Fabio, spoke up. Younger and leaner than Mimmo, he wore glasses and an orange baseball cap pulled down low. He gave off an intense, nervous energy.

'It's a calculated risk, really,' he said. 'For instance this Friday we're going to Genoa, and we know what awaits us there. There's hatred between us, there is a rivalry that has existed for as long as the teams have been around, and we have not met them for over 10 years now.

'So there is a serious risk of incidents, there is a danger. But this is something that anyone who decides to go to Genoa is going to be aware of. It's a situation that each one of us is conscious of, so if we decide to go it's because we're comfortable with that situation.'

Peter spoke up, explained how in some countries, the rival firms talk on the phone and the internet in advance of a game, how they organize fights to take place at a certain time, in a certain place, between agreed numbers and with agreed weapons.

Mimmo looked appalled. 'It's not like that here,' he scoffed, 'it's not organized, it can happen at any moment. How can you wake up and decide "today we're having a fight"? All it takes is for anything to happen in the stadium, the slightest thing, a small spark and it's off, mayhem. It can happen anywhere, inside, outside, during the match, out on the motorway, wherever...'

'What if someone in the firm runs away?' asked Peter.

'We've talked previously about our code of honour, well there you go, that's one of our rules,' he replied. 'If there's something going on, and you run away, you may not get beaten up there and then, but when we get home you're gonna get it. I'll do it myself. And that's it. It's the law.'

Speaking of the law... the Drughi may have a formidable reputation in the terraces, but they've also attracted the attention of the police. 'They actually have teams inside the stadium whose sole task is to monitor us,' said Fabio. 'They know everything about us, who we are, how many of us are there, where we go. They come and pick us up when we set off in the coach, and they accompany us when we return home – some of us are even followed up to our flats and houses. There's often threats that they are going to come round and search your house at 6am.'

If Juventus are the Man United of Italy in that they're both loved and hated from one end of the country to the other, their fans have adopted a similar siege mentality to the Old Trafford club. After the match-fixing scandal of June 2006 that rocked Italian football to its core, they were stripped of their Championship title and relegated to Serie B. (Second place club Inter were awarded the Championship in their place). That they were the only club to be punished in this way has made their Ultras both cynical and angry.

'That's just another instance of Juve and its fans being harassed,' said Fabio, 'because wherever we went, we won. They just wanted a stick to beat Juventus over the head with.

And then Inter have the cheek to sew the league champions' cup on their shirt, they didn't even win it.' He spat on the floor. 'There's always a scapegoat in these situations.

'Ultimately though, for us nothing has changed. Whether it's Serie A, B or C it will always be Juve; and our group and our banner will be present whether it's in the San Siro, or abroad for the Champions League or in Serie B. Wherever Juve goes we are there, we'll be there to the end.'

Danny asked him what the atmosphere was like in the Drughi terraces.

Mimmo had been quiet for a while, keeping an eye on Stan, who kept his attention firmly focused on his camera. Now he spoke up again. 'You know what it's like, when you're in bed with a beautiful woman?' he asked. 'It's better than that. 'Cos there's so many people, and we all laugh, we take the piss, someone gets a kick up the arse now and then, it's all part of it. That's the atmosphere that you get at the stadium, the warmth of all those people around you, screaming and shouting, chanting against the opposition. That's what's great about it.'

There was still something we had to ask. Mimmo seemed to have calmed down a bit and Peter figured that now was as good a time as any. He gave Danny the signal.

'So,' he started, '20 years after the Heysel disaster, how do you feel about that? Is it still very sore, does it still hurt, do you still hate?' All three Italians stared at him. 'I mean, do you still hate Scousers is what I want to say… or, um, do you blame all English hooligans? Or just the Liverpool fans?'

There was a moment's silence, and then Mimmo spoke – slowly, deliberately.

'For most of the Drughi,' he said, 'all the English are like

Liverpool fans. Let's just say that after the notorious match at Heysel, we hate all English fans, and particularly their Ultras. They don't deserve any respect, they deserve nothing at all.

'Among Ultras there is such a thing as respect – but how do you get that respect? You get respect if there's 20 of us versus 20 of you, doesn't matter who beats who, I will respect you. Afterwards we both go home, and that's it, end of story. That's how Ultras do it, you understand? It doesn't matter if we still fight each other the day after, or two weeks, three months later, whatever. We'll still respect each other.

'With the English there was none of that, because the English...' he raised his hand and jabbed at Danny again, 'come on people, who hasn't seen those images from Heysel? Nothing can justify that. As far as we're concerned, the English...' he waved his hand dismissively, like we were beneath even his contempt.

Danny asked if that meant all English people.

'Yes, I mean all the English, even you who are here. You're okay for tonight, just for the interview. But we do hate you as well. All the English, from A to Z, right to left. And each one of you here as well.'

'Okay,' said Peter, 'excellent! Thank you!' Stan snapped his camera off and started hurriedly packing up.

Danny turned to Christian the interpreter. 'One last thing,' he said, as Mimmo turned away from us and whispered something to Fabio. 'Our boy there earlier said a word – *cazzo*. What does that mean?'

Christian grinned. 'In English – cock. Dick. Like – dickhead.'

'Excellent, great,' answered Danny with a smile. 'On that note boys, thank you for letting me into your gaff, thank you...'

He turned to Peter and raised his eyebrows. 'Let's do the slips double lively before we get opened up, eh?'

●　　●　　●

We left Turin the next morning. Fabiano the Fixer had come through for us big time. First of all he'd sorted us with another northern firm, the Curva Nord of Atalanta, who were based in the ancient city of Bergamo, about 30 miles northeast of Milan and a couple hours drive from Turin. But we had to be quick about it because Fab had also sorted us out with the real deal, the major prize. We had tickets for the Rome derby... and, by way of a bonus, we'd be right in the heart of the Ultras terraces, too.

'Which one?' asked Stan as we zipped up the autostrada towards Bergamo, everyone still a little bleary from the night before. After we'd escaped the Drughi and all-but ran back to the hotel, we started drinking in earnest. And this time we hadn't been too fussy about the wine.

'That's the fucking beauty of it,' said Peter. 'He's only gone and got us both. We can choose – watch the game with the Lazio or the Roma firms!'

'I've got an idea,' said Danny. 'Now you may think I'm being silly, but hear me out...'

He was being silly. But we couldn't resist.

The Curva Nord of Atalanta – 'Fighting with the opposition is a way of respecting the opposition'

Bergamo is a contender for the most visually stunning place we visited on our trip. I mean, we'd seen a lot of history, a lot of old buildings and cobbled streets and the like. Of course

South America had been amazing, Copacabana beach and Sugarloaf mountain and all... but Bergamo was kind of perfect. Small, perfectly formed.

'Like Sophia Loren,' said Stan. 'Know what I mean? There's more obviously fit girls out there... but with her everything's beautifully proportioned. She's not got the longest legs, or the biggest tits, she's not even got the most beautiful face ever – but it's all just kind of exactly right with her.'

'Stan, man, she's about seventy,' said Danny. 'Have a word with yourself, son.'

Bergamo nestles in the foothills of the Alps, its medieval old town walls giving a spectacular view of the green slopes and misty blue peaks in one direction and winding streets and centuries-old buildings in the other. It feels like a sleepy little place, an idyllic spot to spend a week or so lying back, drinking the local vino and dreaming. It doesn't feel like the kind of place that should even have a Serie A football team – let alone an infamous firm of hooligans.

But then, as we were to find out, the Ultras here are a little different.

Bergamo's team is called Atalanta and their firm is the Curva Nord, named after the section of the ground they've made their own.

In February 2002 the Curva Nord took on the fearsome right wing firm of Lazio, the Irriducibili. As the capital's fans unveiled a huge flag with Italian fascist dictator Mussolini on it, the northern boys responded with a banner of their own – a massive depiction of communist hero Che Guevara. The resulting mayhem was as much about politics as it was about football allegiance: as flares were hurled and fireworks fired and both firms flew at each other with whatever weapons came to hand, they were like two armies fighting over ideologies as well as football teams.

Not exactly Millwall v Chelsea then.

The leader of the Curva Nord is an inspirational figure. Calling himself simply Bocia, he is a prominent figure in the community – giving rallying speeches at open-air concerts and organizing annual parties for the whole community... as well as regularly getting his lads to firm up and batter whatever opposition will take them on.

We met him on the old city walls, Europe's tallest mountain range behind us. He had shaggy, wild hair and a beard... and if he looked like Jesus, he also had an impassioned way of speaking that was nothing less than evangelical.

'Being an Ultra is something that you get from your roots,' he told us, 'from your family and from people who have learnt how to defend their flag, their colours. Football is what allows you to bring it all together: whether you don't have much money or you are well-off, this is what makes everyone equal once we're around the same scarf, and leads us to defend our city together, defend our colours, our family and our club heritage. And for as long as we're around, this tradition will survive here in Bergamo.

'What the Ultras will do is to bring a city together. It is our duty to preserve the real values of football. Football as it stands today, it's disgusting. But there are those like us who still maintain and pass on the real passion of the game.'

We were all a little bit gobsmacked. Bocia wasn't talking like a hooligan, he was talking like... like a general addressing his troops before battle. Danny asked him how they 'maintain and pass on' that passion.

'It is what our code of conduct is all about,' he said

earnestly, leaning forward and fixing Danny with clear blue eyes. 'It's about having respect for each other, always and whatever the circumstance. This applies to the 15-year-old who ends up throwing up and missing the game 'cos he's had too much wine, right up to the 90-year-old who goes along to the game with a little cushion under his arm. Our code is that we don't judge anyone, that's for the courts to do.'

'But what about the violence?'

He spread his arms wide. 'In terms of any violence that may sometimes take place, this is because of too much love; love for this team and these colours. And so in certain situations we will do what has to be done. If we have to fight somebody, we will fight them and be proud of this. Because this is how we honour the name of Atalanta. People may object to this, and it is perfectly right that they should do so. But we are conscious that the fight is the ultimate conclusion of what we're about, it's the most beautiful thing we can do – because it is the one really determined by our hearts.'

'Brilliant!' said Stan, with a big grin. 'That's the best answer we've had all series. Beautiful! And what about weapons…?'

'Weapons? Who do you think you are talking to? There are no weapons! Fighting between Ultras is not something that is the product of a criminal mind, but rather of passion. It comes from my desire to fight, it's my drug: to show to the opposition that they won't be able to come here and strut around. It's about being proud and getting respect for Atalanta, both in and out of the ground.

'This is for real,' he continued. We were all listening intently. 'We're little people. We really care about this, we want to fight: that's what being an Ultra is all about. People who want to be in the Ultras world should understand this.

Defending your colours comes first. If you are an Ultra you will fight. Fighting is an essential part of our world and it will always be there.'

We'd never heard anything like this. Bocia had us in the palm of his hand, he was talking to us like he was addressing a church congregation. What with the scenery and all it was like the Sermon on the fucking Mount.

He continued, explaining what it was about the game and his club that so fired him up.

'Atalanta gives us wings!' he shouted. 'This club is like a mother looking after all of us, from the 15-year-old through to the 90-year-old-fan. It is what motivates us, what makes us speak out. It's something far above everyday stuff. I mean, what else is there nowadays that can lead 20,000 people to travel from town to town, together? It's football.'

He thought for a moment. 'Apart from the Pope perhaps, but with all due respect to those who believe, in 1981 when he came to Bergamo, there were nowhere near as many people out for that as turned out when we got promoted to Serie A.

'So what else is it that can turn the whole town into a big party just by organizing a few things in the stands?' He shrugged. '*Niente*, my friends. Nothing. Football is everything.'

'Amen to that, bruv,' grinned Danny, 'I hear you. One last question before we go – tell me about your relationship with bigger clubs, the more glamorous sides...'

'We want them all,' said Bocia, standing and looking towards the mountains. 'We'll go after them all: Rome, Turin or Florence, we don't even think about who is bigger. We'll go after them all if they don't come for us. We hate them all. We will also, however, respect them all. Fighting with the opposition is a way of respecting the opposition.'

We left Bergamo with that phrase ringing in our ears. It was a typically mental thing to say – but somehow, here, and said by Bocia, it made total sense.

• • •

Rome! We were back in the Eternal City for derby day and we were pumped up. We'd been to our fair share of volatile matches in the last few months – but there's something about Lazio v Roma that stirs up the blood like nothing else.

Maybe it's the quality of the players. Maybe it's the fact that Italy are the World Cup holders. Maybe… but then let's not kid ourselves. We can see great players play pretty much anytime – and we don't need to come to Italy for it, either.

But what you're not getting anywhere else in the world is the Ultras. The firms of Lazio and Roma contain some of the craziest, most passionate fans in the game. And inevitably, that passion can spill over into violence. It doesn't take much for little incidents to spiral out of control, for sparks to ignite the whole city.

Confrontations happen as a matter of course. At a recent derby a car displaying Roma colours cut up members of the Lazio firm the Irriducibili close to their own terrace – it barely got a few metres down the road before coming under a furious bombardment of stones, bottles, flares, fireworks. The occupants were pulled out of the wreckage, beaten to a pulp.

As the police moved in, the Irriducibili turned on them – and were in turn attacked by Roma Ultras who had heard it was all going off and wanted a piece of the action themselves. What started as a skirmish became a full-on riot involving both firms, most of the Roman police force, half the city and seven hours of running battles, burnt-out cars, looted shops, tear gas and hospitalizations.

Oh – and among it all a football game was played. Roma won... provoking further riots long into the night.

These two teams hate each other. That they share a stadium probably doesn't help matters – it means that on derby days the 82,000-capacity Stadio Olimpico is split right down the middle. They call these clashes the *Derby della Capitale* – because they say they're not a confrontation between two football teams, but the whole city.

We arrived back in Rome early afternoon and it was like the whole city was winding itself up. People were still going about their business, pretending things were normal... but everywhere there was a tension, a nervous energy. Everything was happening a little quicker, a little edgier. And everywhere we looked were police. Every corner held a couple of them, every other street saw a van, or a car, or a couple of motorbikes... and near the stadium the now-familiar long black lines of truncheons, shields and visors. The place was primed.

We were just as jumpy. Fabiano the Fixer had scored us tickets with both sets of Ultras – the Irriducibili of Lazio and their sworn enemies, The Boys of Roma. Fuck knows how he did it, because the two firms aren't exactly on civil terms with each other... and Danny had had this mad idea.

'It's our last match,' he said. 'Let's try and see the game from both ends. Let's start with Roma... and then at half time run round the stadium and get in the Lazio end. What do you reckon? We've never tried anything like it before, have we? Blagging at the highest level. But it's the last show, the last time we'll have the chance. What do you say? Fuck it, eh? Bring it on!'

The Irriducibili of Lazio – Fascism, intimidation, extortion
The Irriducibili have got a good case for being the most notorious firm in Europe right now. Formed in the mid-80s, they quickly developed a reputation for their extreme, uncompromising politics – as well as for their confrontations with other firms. Games would see their section of the terraces behind the goal an angry sea of right-wing banners, swastikas, homages to Mussolini and other declarations of fascist intent. They were known to have chanted racist and anti-Jewish slogans at opposing players... and sometimes at their own too.

And if their politics are upfront, they've become a force to be reckoned with in terms of business and influence, too.

They even have their own radio station. Called 'Voice of the North Stand,' it broadcasts official Lazio Ultras news over all Rome, bold as brass – a fact which winds up their rivals almost as much as it annoys the police. And on top of that, they have their own branded fashion line – so successful, in fact, has the Irriducibili label become, that it now outsells official Lazio branded clothes.

A few years ago, when they unveiled a banner declaring 'Honour to the Tiger Arkan' – referring to the assassinated Serbian warlord and leader of the Delije firm of Red Star Belgrade – the government themselves intervened, banning all political banners from the stadium.

That they didn't see fit to act when the Irriducibili were flying swastikas attracted some criticism... but worse was to come. 'Sure, we'll drop the political banners,' said the top boys of Lazio's Ultras – 'but what are you going to do for us in return?' Their power and influence only increased.

And the politics hasn't gone away. We'd all seen Paolo Di

Canio's 'Roman' salute to the fans – and we'd all seen footage of the Irriducibili making the same gestures. You don't have to know too much about fascism to know that 10,000 men giving the straight-arm salute is a pretty scary prospect.

Fabiano had got us tickets into the Irriducibili's end – but what he couldn't get us was a meeting with the firm. They gave up some space for us... but they weren't prepared to go so far as actually talk to us. Not without their top boy.

The Lazio firm's top boy is a man named Fabrizio. And we couldn't meet him because he was in prison, facing charges of intimidation and attempted extortion. It seems that the Ultras and the club management had fallen out once too often – and both had gone too far for the other to tolerate.

When the Lazio president attempted to assert his authority over the Irriducibili by cancelling 'privileges' – access to the ground and so on – as well as revoking 1,000 season tickets and cancelling allocated money for choreographies, the Ultras had met him head on. They had allegedly backed up a plan to overthrow the president – but the allegations were that their part in such a plan used methods more suited to *The Godfather* than the boardroom.

Fabrizio and three others had been arrested – and his jailing was not being taken lying down by his firm.

How many top boys of English firms have been banged up in the past? Most of them? And what were our firms' reactions to it? Apart from a bit of grumbling and a bit of sympathy, did anyone really do anything?

The Irriducibili went on the offensive. They still turned out for the matches – but there was no singing, no choreographies, no banners, no flares. Throughout each Lazio game since Fabrizio's arrest they had sat in silent protest...

and that silence was in its own way far more intimidating than all the colour and chaos had been. It was eerie, spooky.

The word had come through that morning, however. Fabrizio had written a letter – and the Irriducibili's radio station had broadcast it. For the derby game, this game, he wanted the silence to end. He wanted the passion back. He wanted his Ultras back on song, back on their feet, back doing what they do best.

The city was electric with the prospect.

We walked around for hours before kick off, soaking up the tension, the growing anticipation, the whole place buzzing with edginess and expectation at the prospect of another *Derby della Capitale*. The city was moving slowly, surely, irresistibly towards the Stadio Olimpico, westwards to the river and the bridges over the Tiber. The streets around the stadium were filling up, vibrating to that peculiar matchday frequency; the stalls and the burger stands and the shirt and flag sellers; the shouting, the cars blowing their horns, boys and men singing, arguing, laughing, gesticulating; the policemen lined up, watchful, waiting... As the sun went down the volume went up – and with it the tension, the expectation, the pressure.

'Feels like the place is a boiling kettle,' said Stan. 'Know what I mean? It's a boiling kettle that nobody's turning off... it's only a matter of time before it explodes, before the whole place goes up.'

It was time to meet our man from the Roma Ultras.

The Boys of Roma – 'The actual fight, it's kind of like a black-out: the body takes over and you just respond...'
Roma's top firm are known as The Boys – and their top boy

would also be missing the match. Giampaolo is currently serving a banning order from all Roma games – we met him in the shadows by the stadium, which was technically closer to the ground than he was allowed. Dressed all in black and with a black woolly hat on for good measure, he ushered us down a side street and into a bar. He had our tickets, he said, and we had his assurances that we would be safe among his Ultras, in the heart of The Boys' own terrace.

We thanked him – but we didn't tell him that earlier Peter had picked up tickets for the corresponding terrace on the other side of the ground, and that our plan was to switch ends when the players did.

He was a friendly geezer – he sorted us out with drinks as we chatted, told us he was happy to help with the tickets and all – and he obviously had more of a brain in his head than many of the lads we'd met... but he's also not a guy to be messed with.

His banning from the ground was a clear enough sign of that. But even that held its own, peculiarly Italian story. He cleared it up as we sank our beers.

'It was the 2004 derby,' he said. 'It was a weird evening, it started out just like any other derby, there were violent clashes outside the ground... and then word got round, and people really believed this, that a boy had been killed.'

The rumour spread around the terraces in minutes – it happened before the game, someone said, he was Roma, someone else said, no, no, he was Lazio... he was in his twenties, he was in his teens, he wasn't even 12 yet, it was his first derby, his first match, it happened when the police charged... it was the police that did it...

Almost as one, something incredible happened. All the

passion and hate, the boiling pride and fury across the terraces shifted, all at once... and focused instead on the police.

'And that was when, out of the hatred between Roma and Lazio supporters, solidarity came spontaneously,' remembered Giampaolo. 'Solidarity towards somebody that people honestly believed was dead.'

The word reached the dugout – the players could see something was going on by the atmosphere on the terraces – and the game was abandoned.

And then the place exploded. Riots continued throughout the night – not Roma v Lazio, not The Boys versus the Irriducibili – but the Ultras against the police.

'Later the rumour turned out to be unfounded,' said Giampaolo, with a shrug, 'and me and quite a few others were arrested. And it's still going on, we're still suffering the consequences of a legal process begun in 2004 and it is now years later and we are still banned from the ground, still awaiting sentencing.'

It was a great story. Danny asked him if there was always violence when The Boys got firmed up.

'The Ultra is not violent just for the sake of it,' he explained. 'Hooligans are more instinctive, they let themselves be carried away by their emotions, whereas the Ultras are more selective. We don't believe in violence per se, we don't allow ourselves to get carried away like that, give into total devastation. So violence is not a part of our day-to-day life. But once inside the ground, perhaps it's different...'

'So it depends on who it is?'

'For sure, it depends. At the moment in Italian football there are a lot of teams coming up that we've never met before. So this may result in a clash, or just indifference. It's not like with the Milan, Lazio or Atalanta supporters, whom we've been meeting for years and for whom we carry a decades-old hatred. It's not something that is created there and then.'

Which brought us to the whole reason we were here. Danny asked him about Lazio, about the *Derby della Capitale.* He wanted to know where their hatred came from.

'The origin of our rivalry comes first of all from having to share our city with them,' said Giampaolo. 'When you're an Ultra, you treat your team like it's another member of your family. So it follows that if we all live in the same city but support different teams, we are gonna have diametrically opposed views of everything. There's always been violence. There's always been a desire to establish our dominance and so this has inevitably resulted, particularly given that we're all street-wise people, in physical clashes. It's a territorial struggle within the city.'

Outside the bar we could hear supporters moving past us, towards the ground, singing some strange, uplifting song – the only word we caught was 'Roma'. Giampaolo sat there with his head cocked, grinning – but it was obvious that he was burning to get back among it, that his ban was torture.

We had tickets though. Time was moving on and we wanted to get in there. Before we left Danny had one last question – for Giampaolo and for all the hooligans we'd met over the last three months.

'What do you feel?' he asked. 'When you're fighting – what do you feel?'

Giampaolo took a sip of his drink and thought for a moment.

'At first you might feel boredom,' he said, 'and then

adrenaline begins to rush as you wait, then when you finally see your enemy, it's a feeling... it's like nothing else. The actual fight, it's kind of like a black-out: the body takes over and you just respond...

'I really think it's like an instinct, to me it's a natural choice. Some people freeze when they are in dangerous situations, whereas other people react as is necessary. In my case, luckily, my fighting instinct takes over.'

He grinned. 'Have a good match, boys. Have a good derby.'

Lazio v Roma – The Derby della Capitale
The last 100 metres or so to the stadium were the most intense. The dark, the crowds, the songs, the people jostling, pushing, shouting, laughing, singing... the policemen, the dogs straining and barking and slavering, the searches, the barked questions, the holstered guns, the batons and shields and hard, unsmiling eyes...

And then we emerged... whoosh! Into the middle of The Boys' terrace. In the heart of the Roma half of this stadium, surrounded by 40,000 men directing all their passions and frustrations, hopes, dreams, love and hatred towards 11 men on the pitch and against the 40,000 lining up opposite them.

The noise was immense – the roars peaked and troughed and were punctuated by huge bangs, massive fireworks that sounded like the Blitz – and was matched only by the colours, the bright flares and flags, the hands and scarves and shirts in the air, the smoke stinging our eyes...

And not a policeman anywhere near us. The Ultras run the show here. They make the law, and they uphold it. And they're not used to strangers. We were pointed at, questions were asked... but Giampaolo was as good as his word. Not everyone was happy – but we were okay. For now.

It was terrifying and it was beautiful. 'I don't know whether to sing or shit myself,' shouted Stan.

'Sing, you silly sod!' shouted Danny – and we raised our arms and joined in, scarves over our mouths so they couldn't see that we didn't know the words.

Across the stadium we could see the Lazio boys were more than keeping their end up. Fabrizio's plea for a show to remember had obviously got through to the men who mattered – even from where we were we could see they were giving it everything they had.

The game kicked off and the roar doubled in passion and intensity. Above the halfway line, where Roma and Lazio fans met, trouble was flaring – the two armies barely held back by fat black lines of riot police. We bounced along with our Ultras and kept an eye as the authorities just about managed to keep on top of it.

And then... Lazio scored. And while the Irriducibili went apeshit, everyone our end stopped. Stood still. Stayed silent. You could have heard a Stanley knife drop.

There was not a sound until they restarted – and as the roar began again, so did the trouble. Missiles went soaring over the police... and the police responded. One, two, three baton charges before it cooled down – and suddenly it was half time.

Our hearts were hammering. 'You still up for this?' whispered Danny. 'Let's go then...'

We ducked out of the terrace, Stan making exaggerated 'I'm going for a piss' gestures by way of explanation, and made it out of the ground safely.

Outside was just about the weirdest thing we'd seen in the

whole time we'd been away. In the eerie orange light and against the muffled noise of the crowd inside, the police around the deserted Stadio Olimpico were busy tossing bottles in the air, smashing them on the ground.

The whole place was covered in broken glass, the air thick with flying bottles.

'What the fuck?' said Stan, ducking as green glass shattered around us.

'They're smashing them now,' explained Peter, 'so nobody else can smash them later. They're destroying missiles, basically.'

The policemen nearest us lobbed another handful in the air and ducked behind their shields, laughing.

'Fucking nutters,' muttered Stan and we sprinted through the splintered carnage towards the Lazio end.

If we'd left The Boys in a state of semi-misery and fading hope, we joined the Irriducibili at their half-time party. Embraced as we arrived, given flags and banners and shown to our seats and practically lifted off our feet when the teams came out to start the second half, we felt a little bit shady, a little bit two-faced.

And we hoped to fuck that nobody got wind of what we'd been up to.

'It's nothing personal,' said Danny, more for his own benefit than anyone else's. 'Me, I respect them both, I'm a West Ham fan. But we had to try it, experience the derby from both ends. It's just coincidence we left the losing side and joined the winning...'

He was interrupted by a Lazio penalty. As it flew in the whole terrace rushed forwards at once – Stan went flying past in one direction, Peter in the other and Danny was somehow propelled up and backwards. Everywhere was colour and jubilation and jumping: it took us most of the rest of the match to regroup... and as we did Lazio knocked in a third.

Everyone lost the plot.

It was pure joy, like Christmas as a kid – on too much sugar and too much of Mum's sherry. All around us people were laughing and kissing and screaming and crying and bouncing up and down. Despite our vague feelings of betrayal to the lads we'd spent the first half with, we had to join in.

It was infectious. It was beautiful.

And then Peter pointed across the pitch. As full-time was blown and the Irriducibili started the party again, one half of the stadium were getting ready for trouble.

We quit while we could. We left our last match on our round-the-hoolie-world tour on an incredible high.

Outside the stadium, Danny grabbed Stan and kissed him on the forehead. He held the camera up to his face and beamed into the lens. 'We done it!' he shouted. 'We only went and pulled it off! I cannot believe it. Let me just tell you now. It was magical, it was passion of the highest order.

'I'm a very lucky man to be here and experience this sort of stuff. It's the last show. I did it. I've done it. I've been right around the hooligan world; I met all the naughtiest geezers out there. Nine countries in 90 days. I survived. I did it, mum!'

He looked up and grinned at us all. 'Welcome to the Real International Football Factories.'

EPILOGUE

WE'D BARELY LEFT Italy when the news came through of another derby game, this time in Sicily. The Catania v Palermo match descended into a pitched battle between the rival Ultra firms – and when the police stormed the fighting fans, the resulting riot ended in tragedy.

Officer Filippo Raciti was beaten to death. Another 62 policemen were severely injured.

The Italian government acted fast – suspending all football nationwide for a week, and then banning all flares, fireworks and smoke bombs, as well as the block-selling of tickets to away fans, and finally, most controversially, giving the police new and wider powers to 'control' hooligan elements in the crowd.

It was nothing less than a declaration of war on the Ultras.

But we'd seen this before: governments were always declaring war on hooligans. The only question was – just how committed are the Italian authorities to this one? Because to our eyes, the Ultras are not only the firestarters, the loose cannons, the catalysts of violence... they're also the engine of support, the heart of the crowd, the instigators of all the passion and beauty on the terraces. Lose one – and how could you not lose the other?

The first real illustration of these new police powers, this new war on the terraces, came when Man United visited the Stadio Olimpico in April 2007 for the Champions League quarter-final against Roma.

After Roma scored, missiles were thrown between both sets of fans – and the police reacted in a swift and brutal fashion. They steamed into the English fans, most of whom were not hooligans, most of whom had never been in a firm in their lives. Some retaliated but for most it was hopelessly one-sided. Eleven Man United fans were hospitalized – the TV showed horrific images of innocent supporters crumpling under batons and boots, of men who had just gone to watch a match battered and covered in blood.

Achille Serra, head of the Rome police force, described the police action as a 'justified response'.

Bocia, the evangelical Ultra of Atalanta, had said something prophetic to us about any forthcoming war on the Italian firms.

'They will not wipe us out,' he said. 'If someone has to pay, they will pay. Being an Ultra isn't a fad. It's not something you do for the good of your health. It's a way of life. It's everything to us.'